GOD'FESSIONS 2

Daily Confessions of Gods Word and promises over your life
volume two

'Goke Coker

West African Version

© 2015 Adegoke Coker. All rights reserved.

No part of this book may be reproduced, stored in a retrieval system, or transmitted by any means without the written permission of the author.

ISBN: 978-1-5049-0851-1 (sc)
ISBN: 978-1-5049-0849-8 (hc)
ISBN: 978-1-5049-0850-4 (e)

Library of Congress Control Number: pending

Print information available on the last page.

Any people depicted in stock imagery provided by Thinkstock are models, and such images are being used for illustrative purposes only.
Certain stock imagery © Thinkstock.

This book is printed on acid-free paper.

Because of the dynamic nature of the Internet, any web addresses or links contained in this book may have changed since publication and may no longer be valid. The views expressed in this work are solely those of the author and do not necessarily reflect the views of the publisher, and the publisher hereby disclaims any responsibility for them.

Contents

Acknowledgments		1
Dedication		3
Introduction		5
Godfessions		7
1.	Release Positive Influence	8
2.	Godly Heritage	10
3.	Predestined to Greatness	12
4.	Liberated from Limitation	14
5.	Divine Restoration	16
6.	Manifestation of God's Power	18
7.	Unhindered Progress	20
8.	Cross Over to Life	22
9.	Freedom from the Law	24
10.	Eternally Justified	26
11.	Everlasting Love	28
12.	Redeemed by Grace	30
13.	The Overcoming Faith	32
14.	Divine Direction	34
15.	Accessing Divine Wealth	36
16.	Anointed for Victory	38
17.	Releasing Gods Power	40
18.	God Revealed	42
19.	Receiving God's Promises	44

20. Towards Greatness	46
21. Restored to Greatness	48
22. Joint Heir	50
23. Marked for a Raise	52
24. From Glory to Glory	54
25. Transformed	56
26. Opens Heavens	58
27. Elevated by His Mercy	60
28. Preserved by His Presence	62
29. Burdens Lifted	64
30. Triumph over Evil	66
31. Established in Righteousness	68
32. Established in Christ	70
33. Preserved in Holiness	72
34. Victorious in God	74
35. Peace like a River	76
36. Remembered for Good	78
37. Fear Destroyed	80
38. Reigning in Life	82
39. Made for Dominion	84
40. Supernatural Wisdom	86
41. Freedom in Christ	88
42. Beyond the Curse	90
43. Limitless Grace	92
44. A New Thing	94
45. Divine Enablement	96

46. Separated by Love	98
47. The Oil of Ease	100
48. Hidden Riches	102
49. Season of Distinction	104
50. Liberated into Grace	106
51. A Living Hope	108
52. No Limits	110
53. Posterity Protected	112
54. Heavenly Support	114
55. Abounding Grace	116
56. My Secret Place	118
57. Divine Security	120
58. Called According to Purpose	122
59. Created for Maximum Impact	124
60. Lasting Testimony	126
61. Angelic Support	128
62. Blessed to Bless	130
63. Redeemed Soul	132
64. Brand New	134
65. No Weight in the Wait	136
66. My Shepherd	138
67. Delivered from Infirmity	140
68. Standing on the Rock	142
69. Divine Validation	144
70. The Keeping Power	146
71. Illuminated Paths	148

72. Unusually Favoured	150
73. Due for Elevation	152
74. Season of Upward Lift	154
75. Saved to Serve	156
76. A Glorious Future	158
77. Power over Evil	160
78. For His Loves Sake	162
79. His Kingdom and His Will	164
80. Overtaker's Anointing	166
81. Delivered from Mediocrity	168
82. Season of Remembrance	170
83. Cross the Mark	172
84. Reborn into Greatness	174
85. Redeemed by His Blood	176
86. Ever-Present Help	178
87. Inheritance in Christ	180
88. Seated in Heavenly Places	182
89. My Confidence and Protection	184
90. The Power of His Word	186
About the Author	189

Acknowledgments

I would like to express my heartfelt gratitude to all my Blackberry Messenger contacts who have endured the daily broadcast of this inspirational piece, whose encouragement and response have contributed to the development of this book project, fast evolving into a brand.

A very big thank you to Omowonuola, Adeyeoluwa and Obademilade, my darling wife and our adorable daughthrs, for your sacrifice and support and for consistently giving me the much needed space to pursue this vision. I love you.

Roland, Sesan, Aisha, and Dele, your encouragement at different times have been priceless. The value of your confirmation of the "next step" and interest in the project can never be overemphasized. Thank you for your contribution.

To Jumoke Ariyo, Jackson Tugbeh, Tolu Akinbami, and Steve Harris, you represent a very long list of people who commended the consistent effort of daily confession and its transformation into a devotional. Your responses to the positive impact of those prayers have gone a very long way in the development of this piece and the birth of a brand.

Abiola "Champ" Salami, thanks for the connection with AuthorHosue. John Zidomi, Gbenga Oluwole, and Tiriah David-West, your feedback kept me going when I felt like giving up. Those telephone calls came in at the nick of time.

A very special thanks to Julius Artwell and the entire AuthorHouse family for the excellent and professional services they have so graciously provided and for taking time through the process.

I'm so grateful to God for my spiritual parents and Pastors, the Rev'd Paul and Ifeanyi Adefarasin. Thank you for taking the time to teach, train, tutor, and mentor me through the years, and thank you for the opportunity to serve. I couldn't have asked for better. Thanks, Mum and Dad.

Aslo to Damilola, Yinka and Dayo Sanya, Ayo and Bimpe, Yomi and Tayo, Faith Nwosu, Nkechi, Christabel, Frances, Ekene, Eugene, Nasir, Ezinne, Antoinette, EvaMarie and Japhet, PraiseWorldRadio, Rhythm 93.7, Solid FM, Oscar and Titi.

And to my family- Mum and Dad, Florence Amimbola and David Adeyemi Coker.

Siblings-Adenike, Adebisi, Adekunle "KC" Adedoyin and Folashade, Adetokunbo and Adebanji. I am forever grateful.

Dedication

In loving memory of

Charles Bruce Chukuyenum Ayibatonye Chukuma "Chaz B"

(1962 - 2014)

And

Olufemi Enitan Segun
(1958-2014)

Introduction

Word have presence, power, and prophetic implications. Words have life. Jesus said in John 6:63, "The words that I speak to you, they are spirit and they are life." Words are the only creative force of life. With words we create, re-create, change, prohibit, and allow things in our lives. This is the power of confession.

Words have no geographical limitations; they can penetrate anything and anywhere. A Roman centurion said to Jesus in Matthew 8:8, "I am not worthy that thou should come under roof: but speak the word only, and my servant shall be healed." He understood that God's Word could be spoken anytime from anywhere and still produce result.

Confession means "to repeatedly and continually say a thing in order to achieve a desired end." Confession also means :the affirmation of truth." Anyone can make a confession irrespective of age, gender, race, creed, or location - anyone who desires to repeatedly affirm a truth or a conviction towards a desired end.

There are many perceived truths in the world that people subscribe to and confess, but only the truth of God's Word will make a man free indeed. So when we confess God's Word, we set in motion the power of true freedom in our lives.

Words are more important than a lot of people realize. We must recognize the place that confession holds in the scheme of things. Jesus himself showed us the power of our words when He said in Matthew 17:20, "Ye shall say unto this mountain, Remove hence to yonder place; and it shall remove; and nothing shall be impossible unto you." The Message Bible says, 'There is nothing you wouldn't be able to tackle." The Good News Bible says, 'You could do anything! Jesus is showing

Word have presence, power, and prophetic implications. Words have life. Jesus said in John 6:63, "The words that I speak to you, they are spirit and they are life." Words are the only creative force of life. With words we create, re-create, change, prohibit, and allow things in our lives. This is the power of confession.

Words have no geographical limitations; they can penetrate anything and anywhere. A Roman centurion said to Jesus in Matthew 8:8, "I am not worthy that thou should come under roof: but speak the word only, and my servant shall be healed." He understood that God's Word could be spoken anytime from anywhere and still produce result.

Confession means "to repeatedly and continually say a thing in order to achieve a desired end." Confession also means :the affirmation of truth." Anyone can make a confession irrespective of age, gender, race, creed, or location - anyone who desires to repeatedly affirm a truth or a conviction towards a desired end.

There are many perceived truths in the world that people subscribe to and confess, but only the truth of God's Word will make a man free indeed. So when we confess God's Word, we set in motion the power of true freedom in our lives.

Words are more important than a lot of people realize. We must recognize the place that confession holds in the scheme of things. Jesus himself showed us the power of our words when He said in Matthew 17:20, "Ye shall say unto this mountain, Remove hence to yonder place;

Godfessions

Follow Us on:

Facebook http://www.facebook.com/godfessions

Instagram @Godfessions

Twitter @godfession

BBM: 52D85142

Website www.Godfession.com

Release Positive Influence

Today I speak over my life and my household that the joy of the Lord is our portion. This shall be the beginning of months for us. I command the blessings of the Lord over my life and declare that all that God has pre-planned for me in this month will come to pass. I speak into the womb of the morning and activate the positive influence of divine destiny to release change over my life.

Let nations seek me, let the rich among the people entreat my favour, and let the daughters of Tyre with gifts in their hands seek me out. I declare that doors of opportunity open up. I am empowered with resources to succeed and ability to run through. I have grace, I live in peace, my hope is renewed; this month will deliver its very best to me. I have unlimited access to the wealth of heaven, I am numbered with the mighty in the land, my house is filled with the goodness of heaven, I will feast cheerfully with gladness, no violence shall come near my dwelling, and my seed shall be great in the land.

Heaven will give her dew to me, and the ground will yield her increase to me, my field will be prosperous, and my vine shall give of her fruit. My basket is blessed. I am lifted, elevated, and promoted; the glory of God will be seen upon me. The Lord of Host defends me and subdues all my foes; He shall be as stones of a crown lifted up as an ensign (emblem) upon my life.

I have increase; I am comforted on all sides. My clouds are brightened, filled with the former and the latter rain together. I am strengthened, I am redeemed, I am restored to the place of greatness, and I walk about in His name. This is my season of possibilities; nothing can stop me, for God is my Father. I am blessed, in Jesus name. I believe and I say amen.

Selected Affirmations

I speak into the womb of the morning and activate the positive influence of divine destiny to release change over my life.

My clouds are brightened, filled with the former and the latter rain together.

Genesis 49: 25

Even by the God of thy father, who shall help thee; and by the Almighty, who shall bless thee with blessings of heaven above, blessings of the deep that lieth under, blessings of the breasts, and of the womb.

Joel 2: 23

Be glad then, ye children of Zion, and rejoice in the Lord your God: for he hath given you the former rain moderately, and he will cause to come down for you the rain, the former rain, and the latter rain in the first month.

Nehemiah 8: 10

Then he said unto them, Go your way, eat the fat, and drink the sweet, and send portions unto them for whom nothing is prepared: for this day is holy unto our Lord: neither be ye sorry; for the joy of the Lord is your strength.

Psalm 18: 28

For thou wilt light my candle: the Lord my God will enlighten my darkness.

Psalm 91: 10

There shall no evil befall thee, neither shall any plague come nigh thy dwelling.

Goodly Heritage

Today I speak over my life and household that God is our Father and Protector, Source and Provider; we shall not lack any good thing. Indeed the lines have fallen for me in pleasant places, and I have a goodly heritage. I am sought after by many for good. I am etched on the palm of His right hand; I am not forgotten, I am not forsaken, for God carries me, He bears me up on eagles wings. I am not subject to the dictates and happenings in the world.

I am seated in heavenly places in Christ Jesus. I have been delivered by the power in His name, the power of the Blood. God has shown Himself mighty on my behalf; no evil befalls me. I am victorious in Christ Jesus I am the beloved of the Lord. I walk in love, I walk in His light. My path is set in the brightness of the lamp, and I will not stumble. My eyes behold the sun, and the Sun of righteousness arises over my household with healing in His wings.

I am redeemed from affliction, depression, grief, ailments, sicknesses, diseases, death, and destruction. I have life eternal, I have life abundant, I have peace with God, and my ways are pleasing to Him. I am favoured by God; I break through on every side, and I am not restrained by any force. My days are prolonged. The pleasure of the Lord will prosper in my hand. I have my portion with the great and my share of the spoil with the strong. I walk about in His name. This is my season of possibilities, in Jesus name. I believe and I say amen.

SELECTED AFFIRMATIONS

I am seated in heavenly places in Christ Jesus. I have been delivered by the power in His name, the power of the Blood.

I have my portion with the great and my share of the spoil with the strong.

Ephesians 2: 6

And hath raised us up together, and made us sit together in heavenly places in Christ Jesus.

Revelation 12: 11

And they overcame him by the blood of the Lamb, and by the word of their testimony; and they loved not their lives unto the death.

Isaiah 53: 12

Therefore will I divide him a portion with the great, and he shall divide the spoil with the strong; because he hath poured out his soul unto death: and he was numbered with the transgressors; and he bare the sin of many, and made intercession for the transgressors.

Malachi 4: 2

But unto you that fear my name shall the Sun of righteousness arise with healing in his wings; and ye shall go forth, and grow up as calves of the stall.

Psalm 106: 8

Nevertheless he saved them for his names sake, that he might make his mighty power to be known.

Predestined to Greatness

Today I speak over my life and my household that the hand of God is over us for mercy, grace, and divine favour! Good things will happen to us, for God has separated us for His abundant blessings. I shall not be disappointed, but all the days of my appointed time will I wait till my change comes, and I will not wait in vain.

God perfects all that concerns me. I will not be delayed, I will not be denied, and I stand blessed above the rest. I am a city set on a hill; my destiny cannot be hid, and my light shines forth. My place in Gods plan is sure; my future is certain. I am strengthened with the spirit of might in my inner man; my walls are strong, and my name is written in the Lambs book of life. I live above lack; I am numbered among those who press on to salvation.

From the south, east, west, and north, favour and honour find me. My gifts and calling are without repentance, my gifts make room for me, and kings and potentates will seek me and find me. My star and glory will not be hid; the top of my mountain shall be visible to all.

I emerge as a child of God; the Blood speaks mercy on my behalf. I have grace to receive help. I will not be stranded in life; I have wisdom, knowledge, and divine understanding. I will not be frustrated regarding my lifes issues. Its my turn; I arise and possess my possession(s), and I take my position. I lay hold of the horns of the altar and receive mercy. My prayers are answered, my cry is heard, and heaven responds favourably to me. God fulfils His promises to me. I will not suffer. I walk about in His name; nothing can stop me, in Jesus name. I believe and I say amen.

Selected Affirmations

My gifts and calling are without repentance; my gifts make room for me.

I am numbered among those who press on to the saving of their souls.

Romans 11: 29

For the gifts and calling of God are without repentance.

Proverbs 18: 16

A mans gift maketh room for him, and bringeth him before great men.

Hebrews 10: 39

But we are not of them who draw back unto perdition; but of them that believe to the saving of the soul.

Micah 4: 1

But in the last days it shall come to pass, that the mountain of the house of the Lord shall be established in the top of the mountains, and it shall be exalted above the hills; and people shall flow unto it.

Obadiah 17

But upon mount Zion shall be deliverance, and there shall be holiness; and the house of Jacob shall possess their possessions.

Liberated from Limitation

Today I speak over my life and my household that the knowledge of the truth of Gods Word has made us free and set us at complete liberty. I walk into the fullness of my divine blessings as stipulated in the Abrahamic covenant and ratified in the Blood of the everlasting covenant. The full benefit of my salvation pursues and overtakes me, the ground yields her increase to me, and I profit in all I lay my hands upon.

My thinking is blessed; I have the mind of Christ, and I function at full capacity. I have the wisdom of God as personified in Christ Jesus. I see my way out of difficulties. I have been delivered from shame and disgrace. I have power in the place of prayer, I have the full outpouring of the Spirit of Grace and Supplication, I am assisted in prayer by the power of the Holy Spirit, and I will not call out in vain: I receive answers to my prayers, and testimonies follow me! The heavens over me are open.

The hand of God is upon me for good. I am led by the Spirit, and I return in the power of the Holy Ghost. My renown spreads abroad. My family is protected, and our bodies are healed; the Blood speaks mercy over judgement, and my destiny is not truncated, nor will my future be wasted. My life is secured, greatness beckons, and I respond to the call to be the very best in God. I will not fail, I will not fall, and I will not falter. I enter into my season of rest, in Jesus name. I believe and I say amen.

Selected Affirmations

I walk into the fullness of my divine blessings as stipulated in the Abrahamic covenant and ratified in the Blood of the everlasting covenant.

I have been delivered from shame and disgrace.

My thinking is blessed; I have the mind of Christ, and I function at full capacity.

Psalm 119: 31

I have stuck unto thy testimonies: O Lord, put me not to shame.

1 Corinthians 2: 16

For who hath known the mind of the Lord, that he may instruct him? But we have the mind of Christ.

Genesis 12: 2

And I will make of thee a great nation, and I will bless thee, and make thy name great; and thou shalt be a blessing:

Hebrews 13: 2021

Now the God of peace, that brought again from the dead our Lord Jesus, that great shepherd of the sheep, through the blood of the everlasting covenant.

Philippians 4: 13

I can do all things through Christ which strengtheneth me.

Divine Restoration

Today I speak over my life and my household that the Lord God bears us up with wings as eagles. He is for us. God has spread His canopy of protection over me, He protects and preserves me from every attack of the enemy, and no evil shall befall me.

My head is anointed with fresh oil; I am separated unto good works. I have divine acceleration; I pursue, I overtake, and I recover all. I enter into my season of divine restoration; everything lost in my generation comes back to me. I am destined to reign in life. I will not lack. I will not beg for bread; I will lend to nations. Heaven responds to me when I call. God will honour my sacrifices, and my offering will be accepted. My harvest is released, and I receive the keys to my warehouses. The wind of God blows divine provision in my direction; my days of heavenly visitations are here, and I will not miss my season.

Grace is poured out to me. I am surrounded with favour as with a shield. The angels of God watch over me everywhere I go. The blood of Jesus speaks mercy concerning me; I walk into my era of limitless possibilities. God has set me on high; my enemies scamper into hiding, and they melt like wax before fire. I am lifted above all my foes. I step on snakes and scorpions; nothing will hurt me, in Jesus name. I believe and I say amen.

Selected Affirmations

My harvest is released and I receive the keys to my warehouses, the wind of God blows divine provision in my direction, my days of heavenly visitation are here, I will not miss my season.

Joel 2: 25

And I will restore to you the years that the locust hath eaten, the cankerworm, and the caterpillar, and the palmerworm, my great army which I sent among you.

Hosea 6: 11

Also, O Judah, he hath set an harvest for thee, when I returned the captivity of my people.

Psalm 92: 10

But my horn shalt thou exalt like the horn of an unicorn: I shall be anointed with fresh oil.

Hebrews 12: 24

And to Jesus the mediator of the new covenant, and to the blood of sprinkling, that speaketh better things than that of Abel.

Deuteronomy 32: 13

He made him ride on the high places of the earth, that he might eat the increase of the fields; and he made him to suck honey out of the rock, and oil out of the flinty rock.

Manifestation of God's Power

Today I speak over my life and my household that God has built His hedge of protection round about us and delivers us from all forms of trouble. In this season, mercy will find me.

The testimony of Jesus is the spirit of prophecy. I activate the power of the death, burial, and resurrection of Jesus, His substitutionary sacrifice, and I declare that my life is protected. I will live and not die; my life will not be cut short in its prime; sickness, diseases, infirmity, and their influences are destroyed in my body. By His stripes I have been healed.

I declare that every sealing stone becomes a stepping stone unto greatness for me. I will not be held down by any force or form of limitation. Because He rose, I rise again from the despondency of the past to a glorious future. All eyes will see, all ears will hear, and all hearts will bless the name of the Lord as they behold the manifestation of His power in my life. I rise again to the zenith of Gods plan for my life; I see it, I say it, and the power of the Spirit of the Lord walks me into it. I have dominion as the Lord commands, I am exalted as He decrees, I am lifted as He instructs, I am defended as He has decided, and I am protected, guarded and guided as He gave His angels charge.

The heavens are open to me, my cry is heard, my prayers are answered, and nothing hinders my answers. I have angelic assistance and supernatural support, and I have favour on all sides. I have grace and peace multiplied to me, and its a new season altogether. I have abundance in all things, and I receive the release of a bountiful harvest, a thousand-fold increase, the opening of the storehouses in heaven, wealth on earth, and eternity with God, in Jesus name. I believe and I say amen.

SELECTED AFFIRMATIONS

I declare that every sealing stone becomes a stepping stone unto greatness for me. I will not be held down by any form or force of limitation; because He rose, I rise again from the despondency of the past to a glorious future. All eyes will see, all ears will hear, and all hearts will bless the name of the Lord as they behold the manifestation of the power of the Lord in my life.

Matthew 28: 2

And, behold, there was a great earthquake: for the angel of the Lord descended from heaven, and came and rolled back the stone from the door, and sat upon it.

Matthew 28: 6

He is not here: for he is risen, as he said. Come, see the place where the Lord lay.

Isaiah 41: 20

That they may see, and know, and consider, and understand together, that the hand of the LORD hath done this, and the Holy One of Israel hath created it.

Psalm 91: 11

For he shall give his angels charge over thee, to keep thee in all thy ways.

Job 1: 10

Hast not thou made an hedge about him, and about his house, and about all that he hath on every side? thou hast blessed the work of his hands, and his substance is increased in the land

Unhindered Progress

Today I speak over my life and my household that Gods enduring mercy will be sustained over our lives, and His loving kindness will preserve us in the bond of peace.

The Shepherd leads me. I walk in light and darkness will not prevail; I am directed by the Spirit of the Lord. I will not be stranded in life; my path is flooded by the light of His presence; I will not stray from the way. My eyes behold the sun; I walk into Gods goodness. I am led into all prosperity, I will not struggle, and I part ways with every manifestation of frustration.

I excel in all my hands find to do. I walk in wisdom: there is a way out! I walk the paths that lead to the throne; I see the ladder that leads me to the top. I will not miss my day of visitation. My change is here! I make the switch, my appointment is announced, my promotion is proclaimed, I progress unhindered, and I make the move! Heaven declares it, the earth accepts it, and nothing restricts me!

I will not leave empty-handed; favour delivers the bounty that God apportions to me, the keys to my storehouses have been handed to me, and I locate them all. The doors are opened and I receive the abundance of heaven by Grace: God reserved it, grace gave the access, and my harvest is great. Its the dawn of a new day, the end of weeping in the night season; joy is here! I wake up to all things bright, beautiful and new.

God has come through for me! I break through on all sides. I step into my inheritance without opposition; greatness locates me, in Jesus name. I believe and I say amen.

Selected Affirmations

I will not be stranded in life; my path is flooded by the light of His presence, and I will not stray from the way.

I walk the paths that lead to the throne; I see the ladder that leads me to the top.

Genesis 26: 13

And the man waxed great, and went forward, and grew until he became very great:

Psalm 119: 105

Thy word is a lamp unto my feet, and a light unto my path.

Psalm 16: 11

Thou wilt shew me the path of life: in thy presence is fulness of joy; at thy right hand there are pleasures for evermore.

Psalm 27: 11

Teach me thy way, O Lord and lead me in a plain path, because of mine enemies.

Proverbs 4: 18

But the path of the just is as the shining light, that shineth more and more unto the perfect day.

Cross Over to Life

Today I speak over my life and my household that the power in the name and Blood of the resurrected King has lifted us to another level. I insist that because the grave is empty, I am not held down any more; the stone is rolled away, so I cannot be boxed in any more. My destiny is released from a painful past to a very glorious future.

What was meant to be His tombstone has become the stepping stone to my greatness. I cross over from death to life, from sickness, infirmity, and unwholesomeness to divine health. His body was broken so that mine can remain healed; He shed His blood so my life is preserved. He was cut down in His prime so that I can live my life in full; His life was short so that mine may be long.

I have eternal life, I have abundant life; I am not lost, and I have not been forsaken. Because He rose again, I go forward and progress in life. My future is brighter than my past, and I am liberated from the hold of every force of limitation. Every chain of oppression is broken, my shoulders have relief from every heavy load, and my yoke is light. He hears me when I call and He answers me when I pray. Things are different for me now; things are better for me now, and the devil is defeated forever.

I abound in grace, mercy is commanded, and favour is extended to me. I have the best of heaven, I activate divine release. I move into a season of abundance, and lack is swallowed up. I have the victory on all sides. Things work in my favour, and I am promoted. The good times are here, and I enter into a ceaseless flow of Gods goodness. My head is lifted and my rod, like Aarons, will bud. I am honoured. The sons of the aliens will serve me; there is no evil on my path, in Jesus name. I believe and I say amen.

Selected Affirmations

I insist that because the grave is empty, I am not held down any more.

My destiny is released from a painful past to a very glorious future.

I am liberated from the hold of every force of limitation. Every chain of oppression is broken, my shoulders have relief from every heavy load, and my yoke is light.

Matthew 28: 6

He is not here: for he is risen, as he said. Come, see the place where the Lord lay.

Ephesians 2: 6

And hath raised us up together, and made us sit together in heavenly places in Christ Jesus:

Romans 8: 30

Moreover whom he did predestinate, them he also called: and whom he called, them he also justified: and whom he justified, them he also glorified.

Proverbs 4: 18

But the path of the just is as the shining light, that shineth more and more unto the perfect day.

Psalm 18: 43

Thou hast delivered me from the strivings of the people; and thou hast made me the head of the heathen: a people whom I have not known shall serve me.

Freedom from the Law

When men insist that there is a casting down, then my head will be lifted. Today I speak over my life and my household that God has hidden us under the shadow of His wings and He is our cover from the sun; the sun shall not smite us by day or the moon by night. God is a protective shield for me; He is my glory and the lifter of my head. In the midst of my enemies, I am honoured with favour from the Lord my God. I am more than a conqueror through Christ who loves me and has given me great victory.

I am anointed with fresh oil. Nothing is difficult for me; I achieve greatness with ease. I believe, so nothing is impossible for me. I am up and above, I am where I belong, and my place in Him is sure. I am a beneficiary of the great grace of the Lord my God. Nothing can displace me: I am not under the law of sin and death, and I have been set free from the fear of men. I walk in perfect love; the spirit of fear is destroyed. I am a man of faith; I have overcome the world and all that is in it.

I am exempted from the decay of this age. I am from above and stand above all that is in this age. My citizenship is of Zion; I am not bound by the laws of this world. I mount with wings of the eagle; the winds of evil cannot sway me! I am a fruitful bough; I prosper in all that I do! I cannot be hid; I am a city set on a hill. My light will shine forth in the darkness; the brightness of my rising will be seen from the east and will be manifested in the west. My generation and after will hear about me. Gates and doors will open up to me at will. I have favour. I have peace. I have joy unspeakable full of glory. I have the wisdom and the power of God in me. I have divine health and every good gift from God. I have full access to my inheritance, and I am free from every accusation of the enemy, in Jesus name. I believe and I say amen.

Selected Affirmations

I am a beneficiary of the great grace of the Lord my God. Nothing can displace me: I am not under the law of sin and death, and I have been set free from the fear of men.

Zechariah 4: 7

Who art thou, O great mountain? before Zerubbabel thou shalt become a plain: and he shall bring forth the headstone thereof with shoutings, crying, Grace, grace unto it.

Psalm 16: 8

I have set the LORD always before me: because he is at my right hand, I shall not be moved.

Romans 8: 2

For the law of the Spirit of life in Christ Jesus hath made me free from the law of sin and death.

Joshua 10: 8

And the LORD said unto Joshua, Fear them not: for I have delivered them into thine hand; there shall not a man of them stand before thee.

Psalm 1: 3

And he shall be like a tree planted by the rivers of water, that bringeth forth his fruit in his season; his leaf also shall not wither; and whatsoever he doeth shall prosper.

Eternally Justified

Today I speak over my life and my household that God will disappoint the will of the enemy over us and paralyse all the plans of the wicked one.

God has elevated me. I am justified by grace; there is therefore now no condemnation against me. I am sanctified by the precious Blood of the eternal covenant, and no accusation of the enemy can stand. The Intercessor is on my side, so no charge can prevail against me. They gathered against me in one way, but they shall scatter in seven ways. The gathering is not of the Lord; the Lord does not approve any form of subversion against my cause. He took my place and gave me His. I am eternally justified; I am the elect of the Lord, I am accepted in His sight, and my sacrifices are pleasing to Him.

The Lord is my keeper and my strength; the Lord is my glory and the lifter of my head. The Lord is my shield and my buckler; the Lord is my Shepherd and my strong tower. I will not fear; what can the enemy do to me? The Lord is the strength of my life; of whom shall I be afraid? God is my help, God is my light, and God is my reward.

I rejoice in the Lord my God always. Darkness is swallowed up by light; my path to greatness shines brighter, and I will not lose my way. I am established in His presence, and I have peace with God. I am reconciled with my Maker, and the wrath of God is passed over. I have divine favour with God. I see everything turning around for my good; I conquer the power of the enemy through Him, in Jesus name. I believe and I say amen.

Selected Affirmations

The Intercessor is on my side, so no charge can prevail against me. They gathered against me in one way, but they shall scatter in seven ways.

I am reconciled with my Maker, and the wrath of God is passed over.

Hebrews 7: 25

Wherefore he is able also to save them to the uttermost that come unto God by him, seeing he ever liveth to make intercession for them.

Colossians 2: 14

Blotting out the handwriting of ordinances that was against us, which was contrary to us, and took it out of the way, nailing it to his cross;

Deuteronomy 28: 7

The Lord shall cause thine enemies that rise up against thee to be smitten before thy face: they shall come out against thee one way, and flee before thee seven ways.

Romans 5: 10

For if, when we were enemies, we were reconciled to God by the death of his Son, much more, being reconciled, we shall be saved by his life.

Exodus 12: 13

And the blood shall be to you for a token upon the houses where ye are: and when I see the blood, I will pass over you, and the plague shall not be upon you to destroy you, when I smite the land of Egypt.

Everlasting Love

Today I speak over my life and over my household that this is our season of divine restoration. God will restore to us all the things we may have lost; it shall be sevenfold as He has promised.

Heaven smiles on me, God turns His ears to me, my prayers receive answers, and my requests get His attention because He is passionately affectionate about me. I am loved by God with an everlasting love, and He has commanded His loving kindness towards me. I am the apple of His eyes, and He guards me jealously; He is the covering for my head in the day of battle. I have received Gods mercy; nothing is against me, and all accusations have become baseless. I have peace with God, and my ways are pleasing to Him. He is my Judge; He ruled in my favour, and He is also my Advocate. He took the stand for me; He is my Intercessor and has pleaded my case.

He is my glory and the lifter of my head. He is my help. I have divine acceleration: I am an overtaker, an overcomer, and more than a conqueror. I am numbered with the strong. I have grace unlimited and favour unhindered; I have a ceaseless supply of the Holy Spirit. I live in abundance; heaven assists me in all I do. My feet are led into a limitless flow of blessings; He teaches me how to profit. His angelic hosts support me. The enemy flees from me, in Jesus name. I believe and I say amen.

Selected Affirmations

I am loved by God with an everlasting love, and He has commanded His loving kindness towards me. I am the apple of His eyes, and He guards me jealously.

1 John 3: 16

Hereby perceive we the love of God, because he laid down his life for us: and we ought to lay down our lives for the brethren.

1 Peter 3: 18

For Christ also hath once suffered for sins, the just for the unjust, that he might bring us to God, being put to death in the flesh, but quickened by the Spirit.

Romans 8: 37

Nay, in all these things we are more than conquerors through him that loved us.

Psalm 3: 3

But thou, O Lord, art a shield for me; my glory, and the lifter up of mine head.

Isaiah 48: 17

Thus saith the Lord, thy Redeemer, the Holy One of Israel; I am the Lord thy God which teacheth thee to profit, which leadeth thee by the way that thou shouldest go.

Redeemed by Grace

Today I speak over my life and my household that super abundance in all things is our right. The will of God be done in our lives!

God hears and answers when I call. The Blood of Jesus speaks mercy over judgement for me. I have escaped because of the reality of the cross; my hands are on the horns of the altar, and the avenger of death returns empty. I have been redeemed, and I am free from the law of sin and death. I am a recipient of His grace so amazing; Gods faithfulness abounds to me endlessly. I am numbered among the chosen few; I am called of God according to divine purpose.

My strength will not be depleted, but it is renewed daily. As the mountains surround Jerusalem, the angels of God surround me to keep me and mine in safety. Like birds in flight, the Lords angels constantly hover over me to keep evil from me. The Lord my God is the covering of my head in battle; I am guarded ever so jealously as the apple of His eyes. He has given His angels charge over me, so I will not dash my foot against a stone. He is my keeper, He is my strength, and He preserves my soul and my going forth. My mouth will yet praise His name and not be silent. My mourning is turned into dancing, I have beauty for ashes, I have gladness in place of sorrow, and my light shines forth. Fear is defeated; death is swallowed up in victory, in Jesus name. I believe and I say amen.

Selected Affirmations

I am free from the law of sin and death. I am a recipient of His Grace so amazing.

Like birds in flight, the Lords angels constantly hover over me to keep evil from me.

Romans 8: 2

For the law of the Spirit of life in Christ Jesus hath made me free from the law of sin and death.

Genesis 6: 8

But Noah found grace in the eyes of the Lord.

Isaiah 65: 24

And it shall come to pass, that before they call, I will answer; and while they are yet speaking, I will hear.

Isaiah 40: 31

But they that wait upon the Lord shall renew their strength; they shall mount up with wings as eagles; they shall run, and not be weary; and they shall walk, and not faint.

Psalm 17: 8

Keep me as the apple of the eye, hide me under the shadow of thy wings.

The Overcoming Faith

Today I speak over my life and my household that our lives have been seasoned with the flavour of heaven. God remembers His covenant of peace for us and shows His faithfulness to me and my generation forever.

I shall not lack for any good thing. My children shall not beg for bread, but they shall know and serve the God of Abraham, Isaac, Jacob, and their parents the strength of Israel, the God who cannot lie. He is attentive to my cry, He will show me mercy when I call, and I am established and settled in Him. I will exceed every expectation. God will surpass all my imagination of greatness. I am blessed above the curse, and there is no enchantment against me, no divination against me. God finds no abomination, iniquity, or perversion in me. I am justified by grace, I am cleansed by the water of the Word, and I am covered by the power of the Blood of the everlasting covenant.

I am saved to serve; I am born to reign. I am vindicated by the finished work of the cross of Calvary; I am filled with the Holy Spirit, I am not under the law, and I am not of the world. I have the overcoming faith, and I overcome the world by my faith. I have great faith in the Word of God. My life is safe in Him. I am protected, I have provision, I have His power, and no harm shall befall me. I shall never go empty; I am a change agent, a child of consolation, and a son of encouragement. Good things happen to me naturally; I have favour, and people honour me. The devil is destroyed; God has lifted me, in Jesus name. I believe and I say amen.

SELECTED AFFIRMATIONS

God will surpass all my imagination of greatness.

I have great faith in the Word of God. My life is safe in Him.

Ephesians 3: 20

Now unto him that is able to do exceeding abundantly above all that we ask or think, according to the power that worketh in us.

Psalm 34: 10

The young lions do lack, and suffer hunger: but they that seek the LORD shall not want any good thing.

Numbers 23: 23

Surely there is no enchantment against Jacob, neither is there any divination against Israel: according to this time it shall be said of Jacob and of Israel, What hath God wrought!

Ephesians 5: 26

That he might sanctify and cleanse it with the washing of water by the word.

Ruth 3: 17

And she said, These six measures of barley gave he me; for he said to me, Go not empty unto thy mother in law.

Divine Direction

Today I speak over my life and my household that God has established all our desolate places, rebuilt all the broken altars, and rekindled the fire of His Spirit in our hearts. I have the grace to seek and find His face above all things; I will not forfeit the mercy of God as revealed in the Son.

Purpose is revealed, destiny is attained, and I have the power to become all that God has commanded about me. I can do all things through Christ who strengthens me. I have been quickened in my mind by the Spirit that raised Christ from the dead. My body is quickened; I am strong in the Lord and in the power of His might. I am healed and walk in divine health.

I have divine direction: I have overcoming counsel, the Spirit of God indwells me, and I have the spirit of knowledge and the interpretation of mysteries. I retain the truth, I walk in dominion, and I am enthroned in life. I live above every situation and circumstance in my generation. I take my place among the strong, I reign in the midst of the mighty on the earth, and my branches grow over the walls. The time to favour me is now, I walk in abundance, and I will not miss my divine opportunity. God is with me, and I cannot be destroyed; the Greater one is in me, and every good thing in life answers to me. I will not be denied any good; pain is turned into power, my tests become testimonies, my cry becomes celebration, my joy is endless, and my season of peace is ceaseless. I trample on snakes and scorpions. Nothing will hurt me, in Jesus name. I believe and I say amen.

Selected Affirmations

I have divine direction: I have overcoming counsel, the Spirit of God indwells me, and I have the spirit of knowledge and the interpretation of mysteries. I retain the truth, I walk in dominion, and I am enthroned in life.

Psalm 143: 10

Teach me to do thy will; for thou art my God: thy spirit is good; lead me into the land of uprightness.

Psalm 73: 24

Thou shalt guide me with thy counsel, and afterward receive me to glory.

John 14: 17

Even the Spirit of truth; whom the world cannot receive, because it seeth him not, neither knoweth him: but ye know him; for he dwelleth with you, and shall be in you.

Psalm 78: 2

I will open my mouth in a parable: I will utter dark sayings of old.

Psalm 119: 43

And take not the word of truth utterly out of my mouth; for I have hoped in thy judgments.

Accessing Divine Wealth

Today I speak over my life and my household that Gods good thoughts towards us, designed to bring us to an expected end, will come to pass. I will not end my race in disappointment. I am divinely assisted, and God is for me. Nothing is broken and nothing is missing in my life.

I have peace with God; I am reconciled with Him, God is pleased with me, I am a recipient of great grace, and my faith is effectual: God opens doors for me. I will not be stranded in life, and there is more to my life than what meets the eye.

God exceeds all my expectations; I am limitless in my access to divine wealth. I prosper, I am prosperous, and I live in abundance. I have joy unspeakable, full of glory, and global prominence is my portion. I receive every commanded blessing of God. Every promise in the Book is mine. God is on my side, heaven supports me, and angels watch over me. I am called and chosen by God, and all things work in my favour. I have obtained a glorious inheritance. I am sealed with the Holy Spirit of Promise, and I am liberated to serve, born of God, covered by His Blood, cleansed by the water of His Word, anointed for purpose, destined to reign in life, attracted to favour, and shielded by faith. My mourning is turned into dancing, I am strong in the Lord and in the power of His might; challenges bow at my feet,

I have the mind of Christ. I walk in love: I am holy, blameless, and predestined unto greatness. I have wisdom and prudence. I have a brilliant future. My tomorrow is better than my yesterday, I move forward, and I have more than I bargained for. I am a believer; I have a great expectation. God has my back, and the devil is defeated. His head is bruised; I overcame him in Christ Jesus. I believe and I say amen.

Selected Affirmations

I am limitless in my access to divine wealth. I prosper, I am prosperous, and I live in abundance.

I receive every commanded blessing of God. Every promise in the Book is mine.

Deuteronomy 8: 18

But thou shalt remember the LORD thy God: for it is he that giveth thee power to get wealth, that he may establish his covenant which he sware unto thy fathers, as it is this day.

Deuteronomy 29: 9

Keep therefore the words of this covenant, and do them, that ye may prosper in all that ye do.

Deuteronomy 33: 19

They shall call the people unto the mountain; there they shall offer sacrifices of righteousness: for they shall suck of the abundance of the seas, and of treasures hid in the sand.

Genesis 39: 2

And the LORD was with Joseph, and he was a prosperous man; and he was in the house of his master the Egyptian.

Hebrews 9: 15

And for this cause he is the mediator of the new testament, that by means of death, for the redemption of the transgressions that were under the first testament, they which are called might receive the promise of eternal inheritance.

Anointed for Victory

Today I speak over my life and household that shouts of joy and victory will not cease in our tents. God will lead us in triumphant procession through all the battles of life. The enemy of my soul is defeated, and all opposition is discomfited. I am glorious in victory; I wax valiant in battle; I am helped supernaturally.

The righteous are as bold as a lion; I am the seed of the Righteous, I have the earth as my inheritance, and I have on my body the marks of the Lord Jesus Christ. I am untouchable, because I am completely guarded by the Lord of hosts. I am all that God has called me to become, no stops are on my path to greatness. I have peace.

My hands are strong in the fight: I can bend a bow of steel; my feet are swift in battle, and I march steadily to victory, the song of victory resounding in my mouth. I pursue and overtake the enemy and recover all; I spoil the spoiler and possess all his loot.

I enter into a season of restoration. I occupy my mountain, I walk in holiness, I possess my possession, and I walk in abundance forever. I am a man of faith; the Word of God works wonders in my life. I have divine favour, and I live in a perfect state of health. Mercy and kindness find me; it is well with me always, and I will not miss my season of visitation.

I have authority to overcome all the power of the enemy. I beat all my foes facedown. The arrow of destruction strikes at the heart of the enemy. I am anointed for victory. My haters are turned back in disgrace. I am lifted: goodness and Gods graciousness are my companions, and I have the might of the Son of God. I am set at the top, never to be brought down again in life. I am prepared for the throne, and nothing shall make me afraid. I walk about freely in His presence, in Jesus name. I believe and I say amen.

Selected Affirmations

My hands are strong in the fight: I can bend a bow of steel. My feet are swift in battle; I march steadily to victory, the song of victory resounding in my mouth. I pursue and overtake the enemy and recover all. I have authority to overcome all the power of the enemy.

Genesis 49: 24

But his bow abode in strength, and the arms of his hands were made strong by the hands of the mighty God of Jacob.

Psalm 18: 34

He teacheth my hands to war, so that a bow of steel is broken by mine arms.

Psalm 18: 33

He maketh my feet like hinds feet, and setteth me upon my high places.

Exodus 15: 1

Then sang Moses and the children of Israel this song unto the LORD, and spake, saying, I will sing unto the LORD, for he hath triumphed gloriously: the horse and his rider hath he thrown into the sea.

1 Samuel 30: 8

And David enquired at the LORD, saying, Shall I pursue after this troop? shall I overtake them? And he answered him, Pursue: for thou shalt surely overtake them, and without fail recover all.

2 Samuel 23: 12

But he stood in the midst of the ground, and defended it, and slew the Philistines: and the LORD wrought a great victory.

Releasing God's Power

Today I speak over my life and my household that He who began a good thing in us is able to complete it until the day of Christ Jesus.

The Sun of Righteousness arises over me with healing in His wings; God is at work in me both to will and to do of His good pleasure. Kingdom of God, come over my life! Will of God, be done in my life! Only Christ Jesus has rulership over my life; I decree these are the days of Gods power so I am made perfect in His will! I trade my weakness for His strength; I trade my sorrows for joy unspeakable, full of glory.

God is for me; who can be against me! I have been justified by faith; none can bring a charge against me. I am the elect of the Lord: no one can condemn me, for the law of the Spirit of Life in Christ Jesus has set me free from the law of sin and death. I am an overcomer, and I am cared for I am not forgotten, I am not forsaken, I am not denied, and I am not rejected but accepted in the beloved.

My walls are ever before Him. God has me inscribed in the hollow of His hands, and my life is hid in Christ as Christ is hid in God. My lot is maintained in God; I cannot be dispossessed of my inheritance among the saints in light. My steps are ordered by God, and I walk forward into the very best that God has in store for me. No man shall ever be able to stand before me! They fall for my sake; I discomfit the enemy round about. I remain in victory, in Jesus name. I believe and I say amen.

Selected Affirmations

I decree these are the days of Gods power so I am made perfect in His will! I trade my weakness for His strength; I trade my sorrows for joy unspeakable, full of glory.

My lot is maintained in God; I cannot be dispossessed of my inheritance among the saints in light.

Psalm 110: 3

Thy people shall be willing in the day of thy power, in the beauties of holiness from the womb of the morning: thou hast the dew of thy youth.

Hebrews 13: 21

Make you perfect in every good work to do his will, working in you that which is wellpleasing in his sight, through Jesus Christ; to whom be glory for ever and ever. Amen.

Psalm 16: 5

The LORD is the portion of mine inheritance and of my cup: thou maintainest my lot.

Colossians 3: 3

For ye are dead, and your life is hid with Christ in God.

2 Corinthians 12: 9

And he said unto me, My grace is sufficient for thee: for my strength is made perfect in weakness. Most gladly therefore will I rather glory in my infirmities, that the power of Christ may rest upon me.

Ephesians 1: 6

To the praise of the glory of his grace, wherein he hath made us accepted in the beloved.

God Revealed

Today I speak over my life and my household that God watches over every step we take in our quest for the knowledge of His will. I trust only in the Lord, with all my heart; I lean not on the understanding of any man or my own. I acknowledge God in all my ways, and God directs my path. I will not stray from the mark. I remain on the track.

The power of the Most High is upon me, the Holy Spirit covers me, and the Word of the Lord finds me out. Nothing is impossible for me; I believe in God and in the power of His might. Nothing is impossible for me; I have the anointing of the Lord. Every yoke is broken, and every burden is lifted off my shoulders and destroyed; I will not be unequally yoked in my life. I lay every heavy load at His feet, I take on His easy yoke, and I pick up light burden.

I enter into the realms of divine possibilities. My dreams cannot die; they bear the seed of Gods promise, and God watches over His Word in my life to fulfil it. I am greatness personified I live in light. God delights in me I live in grace. I have the wisdom of God as never before; my ways are pleasing unto the Lord my God, and even my enemies are at peace with me. I walk by faith and not by sight. I fulfil purpose, and I will attain unto destiny.

I am not disdained by people. Heaven supports my cause, and every element of subversion is destroyed. I have good success. My hands are blessed. I flourish like a tree planted along the river; I will bring forth my fruit in my season. I do not lack the supply of His Spirit. I find things easy. I have dominion, in Jesus name. I believe and I say amen.

Selected Affirmations

God watches over every step we take in our quest for the knowledge of His will.

I acknowledge God in all my ways. I have the wisdom of God as never before; my ways are pleasing unto the Lord my God.

Psalm 18: 2

The LORD is my rock, and my fortress, and my deliverer; my God, my strength, in whom I will trust; my buckler, and the horn of my salvation, and my high tower.

Jeremiah 1: 12

Then said the LORD unto me, Thou hast well seen: for I will hasten my word to perform it.

Proverbs 3: 6

In all thy ways acknowledge him, and he shall direct thy paths.

Luke 1: 35

And the angel answered and said unto her, The Holy Ghost shall come upon thee, and the power of the Highest shall overshadow thee: therefore also that holy thing which shall be born of thee shall be called the Son of God.

Proverbs 16: 7

When a mans ways please the LORD, he maketh even his enemies to be at peace with him.

Receiving God's Promises

Today I speak over my life and my household that all the promises of God over us are Yea and Amen in Him. God has been good to me; God is merciful unto me. I see His faithfulness engraved over my life; He shows me His loving kindness, and I am a recipient of His many graces.

I walk in divine health, I have joy, and I overcome every obstacle that life may present with all ease. I have wisdom, and Im victorious in all the battles of life. My descendants are established on the earth. They will be numbered among the great, they will not be slaves to their peers, and they will reign in life as the princes of God and joint heirs with Christ! I am a sign and wonder to many; I am a dream seed of God! My dreams will be fulfilled. I will see the plans of God fulfilled in my life. My story changes for the better; I encounter the sudden blessing of God today, and my encounter is meaningful.

I have not waited on God in vain! God has changed my lot for good. I am favoured over the rest: I will not be wasted, my future is protected, and Im totally covered by the power in the name and the Blood of the everlasting covenant. Life favours me; I am in health, and wealth flows into my barns! I will not miss God. My salvation is sure. My store houses are open; I walk in divine abundance. I break through on all sides! I am born to reign. Nothing can restrain me, in Jesus name. I believe and I say amen.

Selected Affirmations

My descendants are established on the earth. They will be numbered among the great.

All the promises of God over us are Yea and Amen in Him.

Genesis 17: 7

And I will establish my covenant between me and thee and thy seed after thee in their generations for an everlasting covenant, to be a God unto thee, and to thy seed after thee.

Psalm 119: 89

For ever, O Lord, thy word is settled in heaven.

Isaiah 54: 3

For thou shalt break forth on the right hand and on the left; and thy seed shall inherit the Gentiles, and make the desolate cities to be inhabited.

Romans 8: 17

And if [we are Gods] children, then heirs; heirs of God, and joint-heirs with Christ; if so be that we suffer with him, that we may be also glorified together.

Isaiah 45: 19

I have not spoken in secret, in a dark place of the earth: I said not unto the seed of Jacob, Seek ye me in vain: I the Lord speak righteousness, I declare things that are right.

Towards Greatness

Today I speak over my life and household that God has not abandoned us right in the middle of the way to purpose. I find fulfilment in all that I do, and I have good success in all of my endeavours. My march towards greatness remains steady, unhindered, and sustained by the powerful hand of God. I remain in God. Nothing shall separate me from the love of this Mighty God. I am a wonder and amazement to the enemy, because I am created in the image and likeness of God.

I am the temple of the Holy Spirit. I am filled with power, praise and glory. Angels watch over me and every step I take. My God remains beautiful for every situation in my life. I am surrounded with favour as with a shield; I am gifted, enabled, and empowered from on high. My destiny and life cannot be hid; I am a city set on a hill. My mountain is exalted, my horns are strong for the battle, and my fingers are trained for success. I break through on all sides.

Every morning, Gods mercy meets me; every night, Gods loving kindness remains. God is my refuge and my fortress. He is my keeper and the strength of my life. I will not miss my moment. My helpers will find me. My life takes on new meaning because of Him. My future is secure; my tomorrow is better than my yesterday. I have a glorious destiny. Nothing can stop me. I walk about freely in His presence. Its my season of possibilities. Nothing can stop me, in Jesus name. I believe and I say amen.

Selected Affirmations

My fingers are trained for success. I break through on all sides. Every morning, Gods mercy meets me; every night, Gods loving kindness remains.

My march towards greatness remains steady, unhindered, and sustained by the powerful hand of God.

Acts 1: 8

But ye shall receive power, after that the Holy Ghost is come upon you: and ye shall be witnesses unto me both in Jerusalem, and in all Judaea, and in Samaria, and unto the uttermost part of the earth.

Luke 1: 66

And all they that heard them laid them up in their hearts, saying, What manner of child shall this be! And the hand of the Lord was with him.

Nehemiah 9: 21

Yea, forty years didst thou sustain them in the wilderness, so that they lacked nothing; their clothes waxed not old, and their feet swelled not.

Psalm 48: 2

Beautiful for situation, the joy of the whole earth, is mount Zion, on the sides of the north, the city of the great King.

Genesis 1: 27

So God created man in his own image, in the image of God created he him; male and female created he them.

Restored to Greatness

Today I speak over my life and my household that God has turned our captivity. I enter into my season of restoration, and every good thing must happen to me. I am free to experience the very best in God.

It is Gods decision to favour my cause, and nothing can hold me back. I rise on eagles wings; I activate the pleasures of His presence and destroy the yoke of pressure. I am alive and live life according to the grace the Son of God gives. I am numbered among the chosen, and life responds positively to me. I am a son of encouragement; I am a child of consolation. I win always, and my hope is sure! I have received mercy, and so nothing is against me! God has me covered, and I will make it. I shall know no loss.

The heavens have poured out rain on my fields. I have an abundant harvest, and the work of my hands is blessed. I manifest the good and great grace of the Lord. I go forward in life, promotion comes my way on all sides, and I enter into my season of laughter and unceasing increase. The top of my mountains are seen, and they drop their fat. The loving kindness of the Lord blows pleasantness on my path from every wing of the wind. I prosper as He has commanded. I am in health as He has declared. I have peace as He has provided, His blood covers me as expected, and I am guaranteed of an eternity with Him. I am lifted. I have dominion, in Jesus name. I believe and I say amen.

Selected Affirmations

I enter into my season of laughter and unceasing increase.

I shall know no loss. The heavens have poured out rain on my fields. I have an abundant harvest, and the work of my hands is blessed.

Psalm 85: 12

Yea, the LORD shall give that which is good; and our land shall yield her increase.

Zechariah 10: 1

Ask ye of the LORD rain in the time of the latter rain; so the LORD shall make bright clouds, and give them showers of rain, to every one grass in the field.

Psalm 126: 2

Then was our mouth filled with laughter, and our tongue with singing: then said they among the heathen, The LORD hath done great things for them.

Philemon 1: 7

For we have great joy and consolation in thy love, because the bowels of the saints are refreshed by thee, brother.

Isaiah 58: 8

Then shall thy light break forth as the morning, and thine health shall spring forth speedily: and thy righteousness shall go before thee; the glory of the LORD shall be thy reward.

Joint Heir

Today I speak over my life and my household that God has marked us for honour. I will not struggle for bread. I am a child of God, and I am the heir of the King and joint heir with Christ. I am exempted from every evil in the land, by the power of the Blood of the eternal covenant; I invoke the finished work of the cross of Calvary and insist that I am protected. The angel of the Lord guards my every moment.

I am a proof of Gods faithfulness; God has shown Himself strong on my behalf, and I am not forgotten. I am an amazement to many! I am the recipient of Gods goodness. God has increased me exceedingly. He has lifted me this day above all else. I am a blessed man; I am a child of consolation. I am a son of encouragement to as many as I encounter. I have wisdom for dominion. Every curse is reversed and turned into a blessing for my sake.

The fountains of the deep are broken up, and heaven pours out rain. I enter into the season of the latter rain, I abound in every good work, I have every good thing that pertains to life and godliness, and I am established in my place. Gods promises promote me. I move forward according to the promises of God; I have more than I bargained for. My mouth is satisfied with good things. My head is fitted with the crown of righteousness, and God hears and answers my prayers. Ancient gates open before me. I go in and possess my possessions, in Jesus name. I believe and I say amen.

Selected Affirmations

I am exempted from every evil in the land, by the power of the Blood of the eternal covenant.

My mouth is satisfied with good things. My head is fitted with the crown of righteousness, and God hears and answers my prayers.

Psalm 121: 7

The LORD shall preserve thee from all evil: he shall preserve thy soul.

Isaiah 55: 3

Incline your ear, and come unto me: hear, and your soul shall live; and I will make an everlasting covenant with you, even the sure mercies of David.

Numbers 23: 20

Behold, I have received commandment to bless: and he hath blessed; and I cannot reverse it.

Numbers 23: 8

How shall I curse, whom God hath not cursed? or how shall I defy, whom the LORD hath not defied?

Isaiah 45: 1

Thus saith the LORD to his anointed, to Cyrus, whose right hand I have holden, to subdue nations before him; and I will loose the loins of kings, to open before him the two leaved gates; and the gates shall not be shut.

Marked for a Raise

Today I speak over my life and my household that the hand of God is upon us for good and not for evil. God has been merciful to me as He promised; I am marked for a lift and a raise. God has plans for me; I am created for a purpose, and I will deliver on Gods promise for my life.

I am a child born in season; my time has come. I move into my zone of possibilities and enter into a dawn of divine realities. God works everything in my favour. I am the elect of God, called according to purpose. I am born of the incorruptible seed; I am an overcomer, born to reign in life, created to rule with Christ. I rise above the corruption and the spirit of the age. I am strong in battle because God is my glory and the lifter of my head. My hands can bend a bow of steel, and my feet have crushed the head of the enemy.

I live in abundance, I live above lack, and all my needs are met according to the riches in glory in Christ Jesus. I am exempted from the influence of the spirit at work in the children of disobedience. I am a child of God born into the kingdom according to the will of the Spirit. I am surrounded by the angelic host; I am made for the top, I will make it, and the daughters of Tyre bearing gifts in their hands will seek and find me. My help will find me. I have favour with people as I have with God. I enjoy unlimited breakthrough, in Jesus name. I believe and I say amen.

Selected Affirmations

I am a child of God born into the kingdom according to the will of the Spirit.

I am a child born in season; my time has come. I move into my zone of possibilities and enter into a dawn of divine realities.

Colossians 1: 13

Who hath delivered us from the power of darkness, and hath translated us into the kingdom of his dear Son.

Luke 18: 27

And he said, The things which are impossible with men are possible with God.

Psalm 45: 12

And the daughter of Tyre shall be there with a gift; even the rich among the people shall intreat thy favour.

Luke 2: 52

And Jesus increased in wisdom and stature, and in favour with God and man.

Psalm 3: 3

But thou, O Lord, art a shield for me; my glory, and the lifter up of mine head.

From Glory to Glory

Today I speak over my life and my household that shouts of joy and victory will not cease from our house. God will extend my praise eternally. I go from glory to glory and move from grace to grace. I increase in all I do, I prosper and fulfil my purpose. Gods faithfulness has marked my times, and I will see good all the days of my life. I have power with God, created to bring Him pleasure.

I am in health, and the spirit of infirmity cannot hold me down; the cross of Calvary settles it. Surely there is an end; frustration ends. I have divine direction; depression ends. I have joy in the Holy Ghost, and I will live my dreams. I have the power over fear. I have the resurrection anointing, and hope comes alive. My heart rejoices in the goodness of the Lord. I am the recipient of Gods great compassion. God surrounds me with favour like a shield; I am accepted in the beloved.

Good things are happening for me; I am lifted and promoted. Lifes best comes my way; I am destined for the top. The enemy of my soul is crushed. My needs are met supernaturally; God is my source. God will not deny me; I am not forsaken, and I have all I desire in Him. God will exceed all my expectations; I will not fail. I am victorious in Him. I believe and I say amen

SELECTED AFFIRMATIONS

I am in health, and the spirit of infirmity cannot hold me down; the cross of Calvary settles it

Surely there is an end; frustration ends, I have divine direction; depression ends. I have joy in the Holy Ghost.

I go from glory to glory and move from grace to grace

2 Corinthians 3: 18

But we all, with open face beholding as in a glass the glory of the Lord, are changed into the same image from glory to glory, even as by the Spirit of the Lord.

Proverbs 23: 18

For surely there is an end; and thine expectation shall not be cut off.

Romans 14: 17

For the kingdom of God is not meat and drink; but righteousness, and peace, and joy in the Holy Ghost.

Psalm 112: 4

Unto the upright there ariseth light in the darkness: he is gracious, and full of compassion, and righteous.

Ephesians 3: 20

Now unto him that is able to do exceeding abundantly above all that we ask or think, according to the power that worketh in us.

Transformed

Today I speak over my life and my household that God is for us, nothing is against us.

We shall be tilled and sown, and our harvest shall be bountiful. I shoot forth my branches, and I am fruitful in all that I do. God has taken away every form of uncleanness, washed me in the Blood of Lamb, and cleansed me in the water of the Word. I have the Holy Spirit at work in me. I cannot fail. Pain is turned into power; my trials have become testimonies. Hes turned my mourning into dancing, and Hes removed the sackcloth from me; now I have the garment of praise. I have beauty for ashes, I have joy in place of sorrow, and my tongue will bless His name and not be silent.

I walk in the increase of divine provision, and the fruit of my tree is exceedingly multiplied. There is no reproach or condemnation against me. God has justified me. I have found great grace and mercy; my vindication is of the Lord. I am acquitted of every charge of the enemy and freed of every accusation of liars. He is my advocate, He is my Judge, He is my Father, He is my King, He is my Lord, and He is my Saviour. He took my place on the cross, He took my sins and transgressions, and He died so that I can live. He rose from the dead for my justification, and He proclaimed my emancipation. I am free, I walk in victory, and I am a wonder unto many. I have rest on all sides; my warfare is over. I enter into my season of sweetness, divine increase, and great abundance. Heaven supports everything that concerns me. The yoke of the enemy is destroyed, in Jesus name. I believe and I say amen.

Selected Affirmations

God has taken away every form of uncleanness, washed me in the Blood of Lamb, and cleansed me in the water of the Word. I have the Holy Spirit at work in me. I cannot fail. Pain is turned into power; my trials have become testimonies, Hes turned my mourning into dancing, and Hes removed the sackcloth off me; now I have the garment of praise.

Revelation 7: 14

And I said unto him, Sir, thou knowest. And he said to me, These are they which came out of great tribulation, and have washed their robes, and made them white in the blood of the Lamb.

Ephesians 5: 26

That he might sanctify and cleanse it with the washing of water by the word.

Philippians 2: 13

For it is God which worketh in you both to will and to do of his good pleasure.

Psalm 30: 11

Thou hast turned for me my mourning into dancing: thou hast put off my sackcloth, and girded me with gladness.

Isaiah 61: 3

To appoint unto them that mourn in Zion, to give unto them beauty for ashes, the oil of joy for mourning, the garment of praise for the spirit of heaviness; that they might be called trees of righteousness, the planting of the Lord, that he might be glorified.

Open Heavens

Today I speak over my life and my household that this God is our God forever, and He is our Guide from now till the end of time. I will not suffer any hurt; because He lives, my future is secure. I have a brighter tomorrow: I operate under open heavens, I am backed by the angelic host, and the throne of God gives me support. I overcome the world and all that is in it.

I have great faith in the Word of God. I am created for signs, and wonders follow me everywhere I go. I reap a bountiful harvest of goodness. I am divinely protected, I am established, and I have a sure testimony in Him. I receive grace and I walk in wisdom. Mercy meets me, and Gods compassion is my portion. My ways are pleasing unto God, therefore my enemies are at peace with me! I enter into my season of favour: God remembers me, and I am not forgotten or forsaken. God is my promise keeper. He exceeds my expectations, and my heart rejoices in His goodness at all times.

God is my joy and peace, and none can take them away. His love has set me free. His covenant with me endures like the sun. God has shown His strength in my life; He has enthroned me in His power. I am redeemed, and my face is lightened. God is my shield, my defence, and my tower of strength; I will not see shame and disgrace. My head is lifted among my peers, and I am elevated. I make progress in life; my course is furthered. I have the good treasure of the Lord opened unto me; I have the abundance of the former and latter rains. God rejoices over me with singing and with dance. I am blessed beyond measure, in Jesus name. I believe and I say amen.

Selected Affirmations

He exceeds my expectations, and my heart rejoices in His goodness at all times. God is my joy and peace, and none can take them away. His love has set me free.

Mercy meets me, and Gods compassion is my portion. My ways are pleasing unto God, therefore my enemies are at peace with me!

John 16: 33

These things I have spoken unto you, that in me ye might have peace. In the world ye shall have tribulation: but be of good cheer; I have overcome the world.

Psalm 33: 21

For our heart shall rejoice in him, because we have trusted in his holy name.

Romans 5: 8

But God commendeth his love toward us, in that, while we were yet sinners, Christ died for us.

Joel 2: 23

Be glad then, ye children of Zion, and rejoice in the LORD your God: for he hath given you the former rain moderately, and he will cause to come down for you the rain, the former rain, and the latter rain in the first month.

Psalm 16: 10

For thou wilt not leave my soul in hell; neither wilt thou suffer thine Holy One to see corruption.

Elevated by His Mercy

Today I speak over my life and my household that God will convert the wealth of the nations to us.

He remembers His covenant and honours me; He has manifested His mercy and shown me His love. Nations of all continents will seek my good, and they shall open their treasures to me. My horns shall remain in strength. God answers me when I call; my cry comes into His ears, and He heeds my call. God will favour my cause in the land of the living, and I will not go empty; my vats shall overflow with milk, wine, and honey. My baskets have been filled with bread, grain, and wheat. My feet are washed in butter, and the mountain pours out rivers of oil to me.

I progress from glory to greater glory unhindered. As it is written of me in the volume of the books, I must fulfil Gods will. I am marked for victory, I am led to profit, I see my way through, the darkness turns to light at His command for my sake, and I will not walk in confusion. I have power to fulfil destiny; my dream of greatness is alive. I have a living hope, and my tomorrow is renewed.

I am a lender to nations, not a borrower. God is my source, and I shall not lack. Every good thing from God is mine. The yoke of struggling for food is broken over my life; my children will not beg for bread, nor shall they end up in servitude in any strange land. They shall be signs and set up as wonders in this land. My name shall be mentioned in places of influence, I am counted with men of renown and numbered with the mighty. Nothing shall make me afraid, in Jesus name. I believe and I say amen.

Selected Affirmations

My baskets have been filled with bread, grain, and wheat. My feet are washed in butter, and the mountain pours out rivers of oil to me. I progress from glory to greater glory unhindered.

Job 29: 6

When I washed my steps with butter, and the rock poured me out rivers of oil.

Deuteronomy 28: 5

Blessed shall be thy basket and thy store.

Psalm 37: 25

I have been young, and now am old; yet have I not seen the righteous forsaken, nor his seed begging bread.

Leviticus 26: 42

Then will I remember my covenant with Jacob, and also my covenant with Isaac, and also my covenant with Abraham will I remember; and I will remember the land.

Psalm 27: 1

The LORD is my light and my salvation; whom shall I fear? the LORD is the strength of my life; of whom shall I be afraid?

Preserved by His Presence

Today I speak over my life and my household that God has remembered us for good and will bring to pass all His promises concerning us in our generations.

God will neither leave nor forsake me; He is merciful to me and shows me His loving kindness. He will forever be faithful unto me and be mindful of His everlasting covenant of peace with me and my children forever. I am accepted in the Beloved. He that watches over me neither slumbers nor sleeps. He is my shield and my buckler, He is my glory and the lifter of my head, He is my rod and my staff, and He is my crowning glory, my bright and early morning star. In His light, I see light. He is my fortress, and I will never be shaken. I put my hope in God; I look to Him alone, and I will not see shame. God will uphold my hands in His righteousness I cannot fall. I am held close to the heart of the Master. I have life, and I will live. I have the peace of God that passes all understanding.

God is on my side. The power of the Holy Spirit is at work in me, and no man shall be able to stand before me. I break through on all sides; there is no enchantment against me, there is no divination against me, and I quench every arrow of evil with the shield of faith. I am not mentioned among those who draw back, but I press on to the mark of the higher calling. I rise above mediocrity; I settle only for excellence in life. I mount up with wings like the eagle; I soar above the tossing of the sea and the tempestuous storm. There is calm; I have silence in my corner, peace amidst the boisterous wind and the stormy blast. Life has a new meaning; good things are happening for me every time. My helpers find me. God is my salvation, in Jesus name. I believe and I say amen.

Selected Affirmations

I have the peace of God that passes all understanding, nothing missing, nothing broken.

There is calm; I have silence in my corner, peace instead of the boisterous wind, and quiet in the midst of the stormy blast.

Philippians 4: 7

And the peace of God, which passeth all understanding, shall keep your hearts and minds through Christ Jesus.

Psalm 40: 11

Withhold not thou thy tender mercies from me, O LORD: let thy lovingkindness and thy truth continually preserve me.

Psalm 8: 4

What is man, that thou art mindful of him? and the son of man, that thou visitest him?

Deuteronomy 11: 25

There shall no man be able to stand before you: for the LORD your God shall lay the fear of you and the dread of you upon all the land that ye shall tread upon, as he hath said unto you.

Mark 4: 39

And he arose, and rebuked the wind, and said unto the sea, Peace, be still. And the wind ceased, and there was a great calm.

Burdens Lifted

Today I speak over my life and my household that the change God promised us has come. I have not waited in vain; God has responded favourably to my cry. I have my hearts desire, I have not been denied.

God is my shield and my exceeding great reward; He has exceeded all my expectations! I have more than I bargained for. He is the One who answers prayers. I am protected, the heavens are opened unto me, I have the supply of the Spirit, and the angels of God watch over me. God has delivered me from the power of the enemy. I am saved to serve my God; the yoke of bondage and the shackles of slavery are broken. I am emancipated, I am at full liberty, and I am amazed by Gods goodness to me! I am the righteousness of God in Christ Jesus. I am not a slave to sin; the yoke of death and destruction is broken. I am seated in heavenly places in Christ Jesus, far above principalities and powers, and evil cannot come near my dwelling. My children and I are protected; we are sure of the mercy of the Lord my God. I am clothed in power, the evidence of Gods ever abiding presence.

I am a child of destiny, a son of consolation, here to make a difference, I awake from slumber, I go to do Gods will, I arise in His might, I attain unto Gods will for my life, and I fulfil His plan for my destiny. I am a success; I enter into the perfect will of God. My purpose will not be jettisoned; I will keep the faith. My testimony will stand. I will be perfected in Him. I have abundant favour; my inheritance in Him is secure, and I am not moved by what I see. I am blessed, in Jesus name. I believe and I say amen.

Selected Affirmations

God has delivered me from the power of the enemy. I am saved to serve my God; the yoke of bondage and the shackles of slavery are broken.

Isaiah 10: 27

And it shall come to pass in that day, that his burden shall be taken away from off thy shoulder, and his yoke from off thy neck, and the yoke shall be destroyed because of the anointing.

Genesis 15: 1

After these things the word of the Lord came unto Abram in a vision, saying, Fear not, Abram: I am thy shield, and thy exceeding great reward.

Psalm 132: 4

I will not give sleep to mine eyes, or slumber to mine eyelids.

Colossians 4: 12

Epaphras, who is one of you, a servant of Christ, saluteth you, always labouring fervently for you in prayers, that ye may stand perfect and complete in all the will of God.

2 Timothy 4: 7

I have fought a good fight, I have finished my course, I have kept the faith.

Triumph over Evil

Today I speak over my life and my household that we will rejoice in the goodness of the Lord our God and bless His name for His graciousness. I triumph over the enemy of my soul; situations and circumstances will not lord over me. Regardless of what prevails in the world, I have a separate path to being established.

I have divine exemption from the curse of the law; I am a beneficiary of Gods great grace. God is on my side, heaven supports me, I have angelic assistance, and I am divinely enabled. My dreams are alive and in place; Gods vision for my life is clear, and I have no hindrance, no difficulties on my way to greatness. I have the fullness of joy; despair, distress, disease, disgrace, and discomfort are all dissolved. I have clarity of purpose and heed the call to divine destiny; my light shines in darkness, and darkness cannot comprehend the brightness of my rising.

Faith arises in me, and I overcome the world and all that is in it. I am a winner, for God is my victory, God is my Champion. I hold my peace, and He fights my battles; He is my glory and the lifter of my head. I am a wonder to my generation; my sun will not lose its brightness, and my star will shine and not lose its glory. I am the righteousness of God in Christ Jesus. My season of struggle has come to an end, I welcome the dawn of a new era and step into a season of ease, plenty, goodness, comfort, grace, mercy, and Gods favour. All things work together for my good. God loves me, evil cannot befall me, and I am covered in the shadow of Gods wings. I am victorious, in Jesus name. I believe and I say amen.

Selected Affirmations

I triumph over the enemy of my soul; situations and circumstances will not lord it over me. Regardless of what prevails in the world, I have a separate path to being established.

I overcome the world and all that is in it. I am a winner, for God is my victory, God is my Champion.

God loves me, evil cannot befall me, and I am covered in the shadow of Gods wings.

John 16: 33

These things I have spoken unto you, that in me ye might have peace. In the world ye shall have tribulation: but be of good cheer; I have overcome the world.

Psalm 91: 10

There shall no evil befall thee, neither shall any plague come nigh thy dwelling.

Psalm 40: 2

He brought me up also out of an horrible pit, out of the miry clay, and set my feet upon a rock, and established my goings.

1 John 5: 4

For whatsoever is born of God overcometh the world: and this is the victory that overcometh the world, even our faith.

Psalm 17: 8

Keep me as the apple of the eye, hide me under the shadow of thy wings.

Established in Righteousness

Today I speak over my life and my household that Gods grace abounds to us in all things and at all times. I will not suffer or lack things that pertain to life and godliness. I am established in righteousness, and I serve the Lord my God with all I have. I am profitable in the service of the kingdom of God.

I am perfected in Gods will for my life. I will not run in vain. My eternity is sure. I enter into my season of limitless manifestation of Gods goodness. I receive the ability to prosper afresh in all that my hands find to do. The land will yield her maximum to me. Heaven has blessed me with abundance. I have the keys to the kingdom, doors are open to me, windows are not shut from me, and brazen gates and iron bars are broken and cut asunder. My storehouses are open; I plunder the wealth of the wicked.

Nothing is difficult for me; impossibility is nothing. I have great faith, and God is pleased with me. My enemies are at peace with me. I walk on my high places, I am safe from hurt and harm, and I am delivered from the fire and the flood. Nothing is against me. I am more than a conqueror. I can do all things through Christ who strengthens me. I am strengthened by the spirit of might in my inner man. I have divine providence and angelic assistance. This season will deliver her best to me. My time is come; nothing can change that. God is my help; I cannot be delayed, I cannot be denied I am a champion. In all the battles of life, I win all the time, in Jesus name. I believe and I say amen.

Selected Affirmations

I enter into my season of limitless manifestation of Gods goodness. I receive the ability to prosper afresh in all my hands find to do.

2 Peter 1: 3

According as his divine power hath given unto us all things that pertain unto life and godliness, through the knowledge of him that hath called us to glory and virtue.

Isaiah 45: 19

I have not spoken in secret, in a dark place of the earth: I said not unto the seed of Jacob, Seek ye me in vain: I the LORD speak righteousness, I declare things that are right.

Matthew 16: 19

And I will give unto thee the keys of the kingdom of heaven: and whatsoever thou shalt bind on earth shall be bound in heaven: and whatsoever thou shalt loose on earth shall be loosed in heaven.

Isaiah 45: 2

I will go before thee, and make the crooked places straight: I will break in pieces the gates of brass, and cut in sunder the bars of iron.

Philippians 4: 13

I can do all things through Christ which strengtheneth me.

Established in Christ

Today I speak over my life and my household that God has promoted us and numbered us among the powerful in this generation. God has changed my story for the better according to His promise to me; He has sanctified me for a purpose and glorified me according to His righteousness. I am a city set on a hill; my light cannot be hid. I am created in His glory; I cannot be small.

I fulfil that which is written of me in the volume of the book: I do the will of God; I do not lack His power and the supply of His Spirit. I am protected by the covering of the pillar of cloud by day and the pillar of fire by night. The sun shall not strike me by day, nor shall the moon strike me by night; I am seated with Christ in heavenly places, I am established in Him. I am secured in His promises. My position, another will not take. My inheritance will not fall into the lot of another. I am free from the power of sin. I am not a slave to infirmity and sickness; I live in health, and wealth is attracted to me.

People honour me, and favour encompasses me like a shield. I have dominion as God has ordered, and nothing falls in my life. Nations shall come to the brightness of my rising; I rule in the midst of my enemy. I have divine increase; I have limitless access to divine wisdom. The Spirit of God makes me outstanding; I excel in all that I do, in Jesus name. I believe and I say amen.

SELECTED AFFIRMATIONS

He has sanctified me for a purpose and glorified me according to His righteousness.

I have dominion as God has ordered, and nothing falls in my life. Nations shall come to the brightness of my rising; I rule in the midst of my enemy.

Matthew 5: 14

Ye are the light of the world. A city that is set on an hill cannot be hid.

Philippians 1: 19

For I know that this shall turn to my salvation through your prayer, and the supply of the Spirit of Jesus Christ.

Psalm 121: 6

The sun shall not smite thee by day, nor the moon by night.

Psalm 5: 12

For thou, LORD, wilt bless the righteous; with favour wilt thou compass him as with a shield.

Isaiah 60: 3

And the Gentiles shall come to thy light, and kings to the brightness of thy rising.

Preserved in Holiness

Today I speak over my life and my household that God is our defence, our shield and our ever-present help in the time of need. He will not leave or forsake me in the time of need. God keeps me from the sparks of trouble, and none shall come upon me.

I am protected from every incursion of the enemy; none of the enemys fiery darts shall touch me. My faith is strengthened by the power of His Spirit and the force of His love. Not one mountain shall stand before me; I will dwell in the tabernacle of the Lord all the days of my life. The Lord God is my keeper and guide, and my soul is preserved for ever. I am hid in the secret place of the Lord my God, far from the dangers of this age. Because He died I live: my life is preserved for His sake, my body shall not be broken, my blood will not be shed, and I will not mourn the loss of my children, siblings, and relations. I shall live and not die I am in peace! I am favoured above the rest; I am preserved in holiness. I experience Gods love, goodness, peace, power, and anointing wherever I turn.

People will serve me, angels will do my bidding, and my enemies will bow to me. I am established in His purpose, I am victorious over sin, and I reign in life. The law of sin and death cannot hold me; I am seated above every strange spirit of this age, I am too blessed to be cursed, and I abide in total safety. I am a child of the King, in Jesus name. I believe and I say amen.

SELECTED AFFIRMATIONS

My faith is strengthened by the power of His Spirit and the force of His love.

I am seated above every strange spirit of this age.

I am preserved in holiness. I experience Gods love, goodness, peace, power, and anointing wherever I turn.

Psalm 46: 1

God *is* our refuge and strength, a very present help in trouble.

Psalm 27: 9

Hide not thy face far from me; put not thy servant away in anger: thou hast been my help; leave me not, neither forsake me, O God of my salvation.

Psalm 91: 1

He that dwelleth in the secret place of the Most High shall abide under the shadow of the Almighty.

1 Corinthians 11: 24

And when he had given thanks, he brake it, and said, Take, eat: this is my body, which is broken for you: this do in remembrance of me.

Psalm 103: 20

Bless the LORD , ye his angels, that excel in strength, that do his commandments, hearkening unto the voice of his word.

Victorious in God

Today I speak over my life and my household that God will show us mercy in the land of the living. God has made me stronger than my enemies and He gives me peace round about. None shall make me afraid, and nothing will make me lose face. I will not see shame, neither will I be disgraced.

God leads me in His wisdom and I am protected by His integrity. Righteousness preserves me, and my head has been lifted. My mountain shall abide and I remain in strength. I will not fail in life; I excel in the might of the Most High. I will sit with the Elders at the gate and prevail among my peers. I am a success in my generation, and my prominence shall be global. The Blood of the everlasting covenant sanctifies me, and I am anointed unto good works. I am immune to every attack of the enemy because God is for me. The yoke of poverty and lack is destroyed. I move over from death to life; trouble and distress pass me up, and I remain in health. The battle is not mine but the Lords; I have the victory.

I am promoted on all sides; I make progress in every area of my life. God is at peace with me. My soul finds rest in God alone. I am surrounded by an innumerable company of the angelic host, and I am delivered from every snare set for my feet. My eyes are delivered from tears of regret, and my soul is delivered from the sighs of depression. I am a creature of amazing testimonies, favour follows me, and Gods kindness keeps me. I am a recipient of His mercy; in Jesus name. I believe and I say amen.

Selected Affirmations

I am a success in my generation, and my prominence shall be global.

I am a creature of amazing testimonies, favour follows me, and Gods kindness keeps me.

Psalm 142: 5

I cried unto thee, O Lord: I said, Thou art my refuge and my portion in the land of the living.

1 Kings 4: 24

For he had dominion over all the region on this side the river, from Tiphsah even to Azzah, over all the kings on this side the river: and he had peace on all sides round about him.

Isaiah 10: 27

And it shall come to pass in that day, that his burden shall be taken away from off thy shoulder, and his yoke from off thy neck, and the yoke shall be destroyed because of the anointing.

Hebrews 12: 22

But ye are come unto mount Sion, and unto the city of the living God, the heavenly Jerusalem, and to an innumerable company of angels.

Psalm 91: 3

Surely he shall deliver thee from the snare of the fowler, and from the noisome pestilence.

Peace like a River

Today I speak over my life and my household that God will settle us as He has promised. He will not deny Himself, and His promises to us are Yea and Amen in Him. I soar like an eagle and will not remain rooted to the same level; I was born to reign, and so I must.

God is my covering in the day of battle, and He is my song and dance so I cannot be depressed. God is my strength in the times of loneliness; He is my banner in the time of war, and He is my hope of victory. God is faithful to me. I prevail over the enemy of my soul, I beat down all my foes, and my dominion is from sea to sea. The spirit at work in the sons of disobedience will not come upon my children. My seed is preserved in righteousness. I am not created for trouble; I have undeniable access to the throne of mercy.

My heart rejoices in the goodness of the Lord my God to me. New mercies are mine this morning; all day I have the compassion of my God. His love has set me free, and I am free indeed. God is my joy giver; He has given me peace like a river. Shouts of joy and victory will not cease within my gates. I am the righteous of the Lord. Gods mighty hand has done mighty things in my life; I am not ordinary, I have the Spirit of God inside me, I have the life of God, and I have the mind of Christ. I am obedient to the prompting of the Holy Spirit. I will eat the good of the land, He will fill my mouth with plenty, and He will keep His covenant of grace with me forever. I am lifted, I am a blessed man, and I cannot be cursed, in Jesus name. I believe and I say amen.

Selected Affirmations

He is my strength in the times of loneliness.

God is my joy giver; He has given me peace like a river.

1 Peter 5: 10

But the God of all grace, who hath called us unto his eternal glory by Christ Jesus, after that ye have suffered a while, make you perfect, stablish, strengthen, settle you.

Isaiah 40: 31

But they that wait upon the Lord shall renew their strength; they shall mount up with wings as eagles; they shall run, and not be weary; and they shall walk, and not faint.

Psalm 89: 2125

With whom my hand shall be established: mine arm also shall strengthen him. The enemy shall not exact upon him; nor the son of wickedness afflict him.

And I will beat down his foes before his face, and plague them that hate him. But my faithfulness and my mercy shall be with him: and in my name shall his horn be exalted. I will set his hand also in the sea, and his right hand in the rivers.

Lamentations 3: 2223

It is of the Lord s mercies that we are not consumed, because his compassions fail not. They are new every morning: great is thy faithfulness.

1 Corinthians 2: 16

For who hath known the mind of the Lord, that he may instruct him? but we have the mind of Christ.

Remembered for Good

Today I speak over my life and my household that God will complete the good work He has started in us. I remain and continue to be established in His love and righteousness. God smiles on me and continually lifts my head. God constantly assists me and makes my light to shine. I am never forsaken, and heaven always remembers me for good.

I have a goodly heritage; a thousand may fall at my side and ten thousand at my right hand, but no evil shall come near my dwelling, and no harm shall befall me. The noise of violence shall not be heard in my city. I rebuke the company of spearmen and expose the workers of iniquity; I declare that I abide in peace, and nothing shall upset me. My family is covered; my business is covered by the power in the name of Jesus. I prosper and am in health even as my soul prospers. I have the favour of God, I have received mercy.

Goodness is my companion. I will fulfil my purpose; my destiny in God is secure. Things happen for me, I see progress coming my way, my victory is unhindered, and my success is limitless. My life is protected, my reign in life is unending, and the enemys fall is final. I arise and I stay lifted: I will not fall! I will not fail! I am a blessing to Gods creation. My generation will hear from me. I am a blessing to humankind, in Jesus name. I believe and I say amen.

SELECTED AFFIRMATIONS

I declare that I abide in peace, and nothing shall upset me. My family is covered; my business is covered by the power in the name of Jesus

2 Corinthians 1: 20

For all the promises of God in him are yea, and in him Amen, unto the glory of God by us.

Philippians 1: 6

Being confident of this very thing, that he which hath begun a good work in you will perform it until the day of Jesus Christ.

Genesis 30: 22

And God remembered Rachel, and God hearkened to her, and opened her womb.

Isaiah 60: 18

Violence shall no more be heard in thy land, wasting nor destruction within thy borders; but thou shalt call thy walls Salvation, and thy gates Praise.

Psalm 23: 6

Surely goodness and mercy shall follow me all the days of my life: and I will dwell in the house of the LORD for ever.

Fear Destroyed

Today I speak over my life and my household that this God will be our God forever, and He will be our guide from now even till the end of time.

God fulfils all of His promises to me. He will neither leave nor forsake me; He abides faithful, and He has shown Himself merciful to me. He has overlooked all my transgressions and cleansed me in the power of His Blood. He has imputed His righteousness to me and I have peace with Him. Grace is bestowed and I know I am forgiven. I am the apple of His eye and He guards me jealously. No evil shall come near me, no pestilence shall invade my dwelling, and I am delivered from every plague and protected from every ill wind.

I am the beloved of the Lord; I am loved perfectly by a perfect God. All fear is defeated, and my tomorrow is secure; because He holds my future, my life is worth the living. I will attain unto a fullness of purpose; my destiny will not be truncated, and I will not be stranded. I am on the Lords side, His ears are open to my cry, and He will receive my sacrifices; my offerings are accepted. My seed is in good ground and my harvest is sure. I will not be rejected. I am established in His favour. I am protected: God fights my battles, and I hold my peace, in Jesus name. I believe and I say amen.

SELECTED AFFIRMATIONS

No evil shall come near me, no pestilence shall invade my dwelling, and I am delivered from every plague and protected from every ill wind.

Psalm 27: 9

Hide not thy face far from me; put not thy servant away in anger: thou hast been my help; leave me not, neither forsake me, O God of my salvation.

1 John 1: 9

If we confess our sins, he is faithful and just to forgive us our sins, and to cleanse us from all unrighteousness.

Zechariah 2: 8

For thus saith the LORD of hosts; After the glory hath he sent me unto the nations which spoiled you: for he that toucheth you toucheth the apple of his eye.

Ephesians 1: 6

To the praise of the glory of his grace, wherein he hath made us accepted in the beloved.

Luke 8: 8

And other fell on good ground, and sprang up, and bare fruit an hundredfold. And when he had said these things, he cried, He that hath ears to hear, let him hear.

Reigning in Life

Today I speak over my life and my household that God will be there for us and not forsake us. Through the fire and through the flood, He has kept me safe and sound; no weapon fashioned and formed against me prospers, and every tongue that rises against me in judgment, I have silenced. I rise above depression, shame, and every form of satanic plan. I am separated for a divine uplift regardless of the taunting of the enemy; I have the victory over every accusation of my foes.

God favours me in life and I overcome every struggle. I am an amazement to many, born as a sign, given as a wonder. I am on top all the time, I am ahead always, and nothing can stop me. I am created for dominion; I reign in life. I am seated in heavenly places in Christ Jesus. I am a child of the Most High God. I have on my body the marks of the Lord, and no one can trouble me anymore. My God rules in the affairs of men, my needs are met, my life blossoms everything in life favours me. God has turned it around for my good. I am promoted, my path shines, and there is no darkness in front of me. My story has changed. I step into a new season. God loves me, in Jesus name. I believe and I say amen.

Selected Affirmations

I rise above depression, shame and every form of satanic plan. I am separated for a divine uplift regardless of the taunting of the enemy

God loves me.

Isaiah 43: 2

When thou passest through the waters, I will be with thee; and through the rivers, they shall not overflow thee: when thou walkest through the fire, thou shalt not be burned; neither shall the flame kindle upon thee.

Isaiah 54: 17

No weapon that is formed against thee shall prosper; and every tongue that shall rise against thee in judgment thou shalt condemn. This is the heritage of the servants of the Lord , and their righteousness is of me, saith the Lord.

Ephesians 2: 6

And [God] hath raised us up together, and made us sit together in heavenly places in Christ Jesus.

Galatians 6: 17

From henceforth let no man trouble me: for I bear in my body the marks of the Lord Jesus.

Proverbs 4: 18

But the path of the just is as the shining light, that shineth more and more unto the perfect day.

Made for Dominion

Today I speak over me and my household that God will be our covering in the day of trouble and our help in the times of need. God is my tower of strength and my rock of defence; I will not fear. I am safe from every form of offence and oppression,

I have the testimony of Jesus, I have the Spirit of Prophecy. The heaven over me is open. I have divine clearance to progress in life. I hear God speak expressly; I see God moving me forward. The power of the Holy Spirit leads me, and I will not go astray in life. I am guided in my race towards purpose, and I shall not be stranded; God is with me always. I am settled on every side. I am upheld by the righteous right hand of the Lord for His names sake. The Lord will not abandon me; I am precious to Him. I am encompassed with favour as a shield, and my faith delivers me.

I am gifted, I am blessed, I am protected, I have a living hope, and I am satisfied with every good thing in Christ Jesus. The Lord is my sun and shield; no good will He withhold from me. I defeat every incidence of frustration, depression, disease, and pain. I outlive every form of stress-related attack and financial discomfort. I have the victory always. I am as bold as a lion. I am equipped to succeed. I will not fail! I turn every defeat around. I was created for dominion. I rule! I am a king. My story has changed, in Jesus name. I believe and I say amen.

Selected Affirmations

I defeat every incidence of frustration, depression, disease, and pain. I outlive every form of stress-related attack and financial discomfort. I have the victory always.

Psalm 61: 3

For thou hast been a shelter for me, and a strong tower from the enemy.

Isaiah 64: 1

Oh that thou wouldest rend the heavens, that thou wouldest come down, that the mountains might flow down at thy presence.

Psalm 5: 12

For thou, Lord, wilt bless the righteous; with favour wilt thou compass him as with a shield.

Proverbs 28: 1

The wicked flee when no man pursueth: but the righteous are bold as a lion.

Revelation 5: 10

And hast made us unto our God kings and priests: and we shall reign on the earth.

Supernatural Wisdom

Today I speak over my life and my household that God has made a way for us, through the wilderness and through the desert. He walks me by the hand and sees me through the path that leads to destiny. God carries me. My strength will not fail, my faith will not fail, I stand tall in the midst of every trial, and I am strong in the Lord and in the power of His might.

My glory neither decreases nor departs. I wax strong and increase in the revelational knowledge of God. I have the wisdom that is from above, and I am surrounded by an innumerable company of angels. They have charge over me, and I will not dash my foot against a stone. My gaze is fixed firmly on the Lord; nothing shall offend me. I am a man of peace. God has numbered me with the strong, and nothing is against me. I am destined for greatness.

I move into the prepared place. Good things must happen to me. The commanded blessing of life eternal is mine. Life abundant will not elude me. All the blessings of God that accompany salvation locate me today. I remain in my place, and I am established in my position. I have great grace. I see myself where God sees me. I am at the top, in Jesus name. I believe and I say amen.

Selected Affirmations

I wax strong and increase in the revelational knowledge of God. I have the wisdom that is from above.

All the blessings of God that accompany salvation locate me today.

Isaiah 43: 19

Behold, I will do a new thing; now it shall spring forth; shall ye not know it? I will even make a way in the wilderness, and rivers in the desert.

Isaiah 46: 4

And even to your old age I am he; and even to hoar hairs will I carry you: I have made, and I will bear; even I will carry, and will deliver you.

Psalm 91: 12

They shall bear thee up in their hands, lest thou dash thy foot against a stone.

Titus 3: 7

That being justified by his grace, we should be made heirs according to the hope of eternal life.

Exodus 23: 20

Behold, I send an Angel before thee, to keep thee in the way, and to bring thee into the place which I have prepared.

Freedom in Christ

Today I speak over my life and my household that God has lifted His countenance upon us and has been faithful to us. I rejoice in the Lord always, my God shows me His loving kindness at all times, and He is faithful to me. I will not be dismayed; I am beyond the curse because I am blessed of God.

He is my fortress; I can never be shaken, for my heart trusts in Him. Affliction, sorrow, and disease are taken out of the way; I am a new creature in Christ. I have the authority, I trample on snakes and scorpions, I have overcome all the power of the enemy, and nothing can hurt me. I am born free; I have been set free by the Son of God. I am free indeed. I am free to excel in every area of my life: I am free to advance and progress; I am free to become all that God has called me to be; I am free to attain unto purpose and fulfil my destiny. No hindrance is on my path.

I awake to the reality of my new status and to the brightness of my rising in Christ. God is my source of all. Lack is far removed from me. The Lord is my shield and my exceeding great reward. I see my promises fulfilled, I see my future established, and I see my dreams come true. I see God change the story of my life. I am not held back. I am not restrained in any way. I am not constrained by any force of limitation. Gods Word delivers me. I am anointed by God, in Jesus name. I believe and I say amen.

Selected Affirmations

I am a new creature in Him; I awake to the reality of my new status

I am free to excel in every area of my life.

Numbers 6: 26

The Lord lift up his countenance upon thee, and give thee peace.

Psalm 36: 10

O continue thy lovingkindness unto them that know thee; and thy righteousness to the upright in heart.

1 John 4: 4

Ye are of God, little children, and have overcome them: because greater is he that is in you, than he that is in the world.

Psalm 89: 20

I have found David my servant; with my holy oil have I anointed him. .

Genesis 15: 1

After these things the word of the Lord came unto Abram in a vision, saying, Fear not, Abram: I am thy shield, and thy exceeding great reward.

Beyond the Curse

Today I speak over my life and my household that God will show Himself strong on our behalf.

I have seen His goodness in the land of the living. I suffer no form of mishap, neither will I be stranded in life. God is my support and my strong tower at all times. He is my mighty fortress, the rock that is higher than I; I will not be disappointed. I am engraved on His palms; He is mindful of me, I am special to Him, and He perfects everything that concerns me. I am not afraid, for I am loved perfectly by the God of the universe.

I am *not* under the Law of sin and death; I am a recipient of His eternal mercy. I am passed from death to life. I have received grace from the Father. I am not condemned, He took the fall for me, He covered me by the power in His Blood, and He qualified me. Now I am free; now I have all the benefits of righteousness and salvation. I am healed, I live in divine health, I have long life, and I have the grace of abundant life. I am the recipient of the grace of eternal life, grace so amazing: I have been forgiven, accepted in the beloved.

God has favoured me; my ways please him, so my enemies are at peace with me; I have received comfort on all sides. I dwell in the loving kindness of God that is transgenerational, and everything I have ever lost is restored to me abundantly. I have power over sin and death. I walk in diverse blessings; the yoke is broken, and all curses are reversed. I am the redeemed of the Lord. Everything works for my good, in Jesus name. I believe and I say amen.

Selected Affirmations

I am *n* under the Law of sin and death; I am a recipient of His eternal mercy.

Psalm 27: 13

I had fainted, unless I had believed to see the goodness of the Lord in the land of the living.

Psalm 61: 2

From the end of the earth I will cry unto thee, when my heart is overwhelmed; lead me to the rock that is higher than I.

Psalm 138: 8

The LORD will perfect that which concerneth me; thy mercy, O LORD, endureth forever: forsake not the works of thine own hands.

Romans 8: 2

For the law of the Spirit of life in Christ Jesus has made me free from the law of sin and death.

Psalm 71: 21

Thou shalt increase my greatness, and comfort me on every side.

Limitless Grace

Today I speak over my life and my household that God has anointed us with the oil of ease. Nothing can be difficult for me, for the force of creation is at work for me. I have the knowledge of witty inventions. I am a solution provider to humankind. I have the mind of Christ; wisdom directs me to profit and prosper.

I am a child of promise, I am a son of consolation, and I bring hope to many. I am a child of light; darkness has no part in me. The Greater One lives inside me, and the grace of God at work in my life is limitless. I bring succour unto many. I will not walk in darkness. I am the light of the world; I am the salt of the earth. My glory cannot be hid. The brightness of my rising cannot be denied. My path shines brighter to a perfect day; I am the righteousness of God in Christ Jesus. My best days are ahead of me; my tomorrow is better than my yesterday.

God is my deliverer, I am not bound, and I enter into my season of double blessedness. I will not miss God; heaven supports me. I will not be frustrated; I receive the supernatural release of an unstoppable and very mighty harvest of Gods goodness. I am ahead of the enemy at all times. I am promoted! I am lifted! I am elevated! I am favoured! I am established in my place, and I grow in spirit, wisdom, and grace. I increase on all sides and in all the areas of my life. I have joy unspeakable and laughter unquenchable, in Jesus name. I believe and I say amen.

Selected Affirmations

Nothing can be difficult for me, for the force of creation is at work in me. I have the knowledge of witty inventions. I am a solution provider to humankind. I have the mind of Christ; wisdom directs me to profit and prosper.

Philippians 2: 13

For it is God which worketh in you both to will and to do of his good pleasure.

1 Corinthians 2: 16

For who hath known the mind of the Lord, that he may instruct him? But we have the mind of Christ.

Isaiah 48: 17

Thus saith the Lord, thy Redeemer, the Holy One of Israel; I am the Lord thy God which teacheth thee to profit, which leadeth thee by the way thou shouldest go.

Isaiah 61: 7

For your shame ye shall have double; and for confusion they shall rejoice in their portion: therefore in their land they shall possess double: everlasting joy shall be unto them.

Psalm 126: 2

Then was our mouth filled with laughter, and our tongue with singing: then said they among the heathen, The Lord hath done great things for them.

A New Thing

Today I speak over my life and my household that God has done a new thing in our lives. My testimonies will not fade away, and my victories shall never cease. Gods glory shines over my life, and I have been lifted eternally.

I forever prosper in all my hands find to do. My success is unending, and my progress is limitless. God has shown me mercy, I have received favour, and I move forward, never to be stagnated. Of my increase in life, grace, and faith there shall be no end. I am jet-propelled into destiny. I grow deeper in the knowledge and the revelation of God. I am established in His will. The Blood of His everlasting covenant speaks mercy on my behalf. Death is swallowed up in victory. Perfect love has cast out fear. I am the beloved of the Lord, sanctified unto good works. I am anointed to excel in life.

I have an eternity with God. I attract greatness. I have peace; I am strengthened with might in my inner man. I exchange weakness for the power of His Spirit. I move up to a higher level, I progress to another dimension. The future opens up to me. My harvest is unstoppable. I enter into my season of unhindered greatness. I overcome the world. My faith will not fail. I am destined to eat the good of the land. I am prepared to reign in life. Abundance is here, and the windows of heaven are opened. The gates of poverty are broken. I have access into the storehouses of eternal prosperity. My place in Christ is secured. My inheritance is preserved. My lot is maintained. God has settled me, in Jesus name. I believe and I say amen.

Selected Affirmations

Of my increase in life, grace, and faith there shall be no end.

The Blood of His everlasting covenant speaks mercy on my behalf. Death is swallowed up in victory. Perfect love has cast out fear.

Isaiah 43: 19

Behold, I will do a new thing; now it shall spring forth; shall ye not know it? I will even make a way in the wilderness, and rivers in the desert.

Psalm 1: 3

And he shall be like a tree planted by the rivers of water, that bringeth forth his fruit in his season; his leaf also shall not wither; and whatsoever he doeth shall prosper.

Hebrews 12: 2

Looking unto Jesus the author and finisher of our faith; who for the joy that was set before him endured the cross, despising the shame, and is set down at the right hand of the throne of God.

2 Corinthians 12: 9

And he said unto me, My grace is sufficient for thee: for my strength is made perfect in weakness. Most gladly therefore will I rather glory in my infirmities, that the power of Christ may rest upon me.

Isaiah 1: 19

If ye be willing and obedient, ye shall eat the good of the land.

Divine Enablement

Today I speak over my life and over my household that God watches over us to keep us in safety.

No weapon formed or fashioned against me shall be able to prosper; God is my keeper, and He is my strength. God is my help; I shall not be dismayed. My boughs shall reach over the walls, and my feet have been planted from sea to sea. I have global prominence. I am lifted above every situation and circumstance that surrounds me. I am established over every plan and limitation of darkness. I am set at liberty to find full expression in purpose. My pain is turned into power, my tests have become testimonies, and my life is a point of reference to the glory of the Lord.

My tents are enlarged. My borders are widened. I have the keys of the kingdom; I have the wisdom of the ancient; I have the tongue of the learned. The heavens are opened to me, my prayers are heard by God, and my requests are granted. I am healed, and I remain in health. I have good success; my ways are prosperous. Life favours me. I am a sign and wonder unto many. I am divinely enabled. I am reconciled with God, God is at peace with me, and I am blessed wherever I go, in Jesus name. I believe and I say amen.

Selected Affirmations

I am established over every plan and limitation of darkness. I am set at liberty to find full expression in purpose.

I have the wisdom of the ancient; I have the tongue of the learned.

Psalm 4: 8

I will both lay me down in peace, and sleep: for thou, LORD only makest me dwell in safety.

Genesis 49: 22

Joseph is a fruitful bough, even a fruitful bough by a well; whose branches run over the wall.

Daniel 1: 17

As for these four children, God gave them knowledge and skill in all learning and wisdom: and Daniel had understanding in all visions and dreams.

Isaiah 50: 4

The Lord GOD hath given me the tongue of the learned, that I should know how to speak a word in season to him that is weary: he wakeneth morning by morning, he wakeneth mine ear to hear as the learned.

2 Corinthians 5: 18

And all things are of God, who hath reconciled us to himself by Jesus Christ, and hath given to us the ministry of reconciliation.

Separated by Love

Today I speak over my life and my household that God has delivered us by the power of His love. His loving kindness separates me for an eternal lift and elevation; I am set apart for distinction, I am marked for greatness, and I have crossed over into my season of increase. Because God is on my side, I will never be stranded. He is my ever-present help in the time of trouble; I will never be frustrated another day in my life.

Surely there is an end; my expectation shall not be cut off. I have limitless possibilities in my God. Everything works for me: I am destined for honour, I have the best of all seasons, abundant life is my portion, and eternal life is my lot. I am favoured wherever I go! People seek me out to do good to me. Gods Word is upon me, I have angelic assistance, and I have divine help. I am guided by the Holy Spirit of God; I have divine direction, I am a child of Light, and I do not walk in darkness. I am the salt of the earth; I am the light of the world. I shine like the brightness of the morning sun.

I walk in the strength of the Almighty God. I am gifted without repentance, I am called according to purpose. I am a child of promise, I take my place, and I am established in the covenant. I break forth. I am not held back. The earth yields of her increase to me, the Nations bow at my presence, I have the support of heaven. And I prosper in all my hands find to do. I am blessed of God; there is nothing against me, in Jesus name. I believe and I say amen.

Selected Affirmations

I am gifted without repentance

I have limitless possibilities in my God. Everything works for me.

Jeremiah 31: 3

The LORD hath appeared of old unto me, saying, Yea, I have loved thee with an everlasting love: therefore with lovingkindness have I drawn thee.

Genesis 12: 2

And I will make of thee a great nation, and I will bless thee, and make thy name great; and thou shall be a blessing.

Romans 8: 28

And we know that all things work together for good to them that love God, to them who are the called according to his purpose.

Matthew 5: 13

Ye are the salt of the earth: but if the salt have lost his savour, wherewith shall it be salted? It is thenceforth good for nothing, but to be cast out, and to be trodden under foot of men.

Psalm 67: 6

Then shall the earth yield her increase; and God, even our own God, shall bless us.

The Oil of Ease

Today I speak over my life and my household that shouts of joy and victory will not cease from our abode. God has crowned my life with grace and granted me the oil of ease; nothing will be impossible or difficult for me. I walk in the fullness of my God-given privileges and divine enablement.

God has commanded good concerning me; evil will not find expression in my life. I insist that God will cover me from the noisome pestilence as He has promised; the influence of the Blood of the eternal covenant delivers the fulfilment of the will of God over my life. My success is divine, my destiny is intact, my purpose is assured, and divine health is guaranteed. Gods love is unflinching, and His loving kindness is transgenerational, so I am set apart from the rest and excel in all I do. I prosper in all I lay my hands on. I am exempted from every evil, and the snare of the fowler will not catch me and my children. I go forward; there are no stumbling blocks around me.

I turn my pain into power, my tests become testimonies, and every prayer point becomes a point of praise. God has done well by me; my eyes will see good. Mercy and grace have found me, goodness and favour follow me, and my helpers come to me. My peculiar issues become powerful points for the manifestation of divine power. My story has changed for the better, in Jesus name. I believe and I say amen.

SELECTED AFFIRMATIONS

God has crowned my life with grace and granted me the oil of ease; nothing will be impossible or difficult for me.

I insist that God will cover me from the noisome pestilence as He has promised; the influence of the Blood of the eternal covenant delivers the fulfilment of the will of God over my life.

Psalm 5: 11

But let all those that put their trust in thee rejoice: let them ever shout for joy, because thou defendest them: let them also that love thy name be joyful in thee.

Luke 1: 37

For with God, nothing shall be impossible.

Isaiah 53: 5

But he was wounded for our transgressions, he was bruised for our iniquities: the chastisement of our peace was upon him; and with his stripes we are healed.

Psalm 91: 3

Surely he shall deliver thee from the snare of the fowler, and from the noisome pestilence.

Psalm 23: 6

Surely goodness and mercy shall follow me all the days of my life: and I will dwell in the house of the LORD for ever.

Hidden Riches

Today I speak over my life and my household that God has lifted our heads in the midst of troubled days and filled our mouths with laughter. I will see no evil, neither will I be confounded in life. My path has been filled with the fat of the land, and I will enjoy the blessings of the Lord in the land of the living.

God has carried me over troubled waters and delivered me from every noisome pestilence. My feet are washed in butter; the rock yields to me rivers of oil. The fountains of the deep are broken up, and I shatter the wells of water hidden in the core of the earth. I locate hidden riches of the secret places and discover uncommon treasure. I have access to the knowledge of witty inventions. I encounter supernatural wisdom. I have the mind of Christ. I have the knowledge of the aged.

The keys of the kingdom are delivered to me; I have the supply of the Spirit. God has favoured me; I have wisdom the enemy cannot resist or gainsay. I am a marvel to many; the world will feel my impact. I am designed to attain a purpose. I attract greatness. Goodness and mercy, grace and peace are indicators of my days. Kings will come to the brightness of my rising. My lifting is constant; it knows no end. I am on top. God has set me apart for perpetual promotion, in Jesus name. I believe and I say amen.

Selected Affirmations

I locate hidden riches of the secret places and discover uncommon treasure.

Goodness and mercy, grace and peace are indicators of my days.

Psalm 126: 2

Then was our mouth filled with laughter, and our tongue with singing: then said they among the heathen, The LORD hath done great things for them.

Isaiah 1: 19

If ye be willing and obedient, ye shall eat the good of the land.

Job 29: 6

When I washed my steps with butter, and the rock poured me out rivers of oil.

Isaiah 45: 3

And I will give thee the treasures of darkness, and hidden riches of secret places, that thou mayest know that I, the LORD, which call thee by thy name, am the God of Israel.

Isaiah 60: 3

And the Gentiles shall come to thy light, and kings to the brightness of thy rising.

Season of Distinction

Today I speak over my life and household that nothing shall be difficult or impossible for us to attain according to Gods purpose for us. I will not work in vain; doors open up for me, I maximize every opportunity life presents to me, I will not fail, I am born a success, I make the mark. I exceed all expectations; I enter gracefully into my season of unlimited distinction. I take giant strides into unusual attainments and tremendous achievements, and I leap into the fullness of Gods joy by His grace.

God is my source; nothing is missing and nothing is broken in my life. I am fortified by the power of His might, and I am energized by the strength of His Spirit. I walk in love; there is no fear in me. God is my portion and my lot. God is my inheritance; He is my exceeding great reward. My life is safe and secure. The Blood of His everlasting covenant speaks mercy on my behalf; the enemy is beaten back into an eternal retreat, and my foes are defeated forever.

He has given me an undeniable victory. My mouth is filled with good things. My vats overflow with the abundance of His household. I have unhindered access to the storehouses of heaven, in Jesus name. I believe and I say amen.

Selected Affirmations

I take giant strides into unusual attainments and tremendous achievements, and I leap into the fullness of Gods joy by His grace.

Luke 1: 37

For with God nothing shall be impossible.

Acts 16: 26

And suddenly there was a great earthquake, so that the foundations of the prison were shaken: and immediately all the doors were opened, and every ones bands were loosed.

Hebrews 12: 24

And to Jesus the mediator of the new covenant, and to the blood of sprinkling, that speaketh better things than that of Abel.

1 John 4: 16

And we have known and believed the love that God has for us.**God is love**, and he who abides in love abides in God, and God in him.

1 Corinthians 15: 57

But thanks be to God, which giveth us the victory through our Lord Jesus Christ.

Liberated into Grace

Today I speak over my life and over my household that God turns His ears to our every cry and answers our requests.

God has turned my captivity and has released the full implication of His mercy over me! God is gracious to me; I have the supply of the Spirit of the living God. I have divine direction; my expectation cannot be cut off. I have answers to my prayers and supplications. God is faithful to me; He has not called me to seek Him in vain. My horn is exalted like that of the unicorn. I break through every wall of demarcation; I will not be kept away from the fullness of Gods blessings for my life. Every promise in the book is mine. I am liberated to enjoy the goodness of Gods miraculous provision. The earth gives of her best to me.

I am accepted in the beloved. I will not be rejected. God is pleased with me. The Blood of Jesus speaks mercy on my behalf, I am justified. There is no condemnation against me; I have been commended to God by the power of His spoken word. God is my source, I am provided for. The works of my hands are blessed. I have wisdom to excel. I am sought after by the mighty. I am a blessing to as many as I come across. My generation will hear from me. My change has come. God has lifted me. I will never see disgrace, in Jesus name. I believe and I say amen.

SELECTED AFFIRMATIONS

I break through every wall of demarcation; I will not be kept away from the fullness of Gods blessings for my life.

I am a blessing to as many as I come across.

I am liberated to enjoy the goodness of Gods miraculous provision.

Psalm 126: 1

When the LORD turned again the captivity of Zion, we were like them that dream.

Philippians 1: 19

For I know that this shall turn to my salvation through your prayer, and the supply of the Spirit of Jesus Christ

Psalm 92: 10

But my horn shalt thou exalt like the horn of an unicorn: I shall be anointed with fresh oil.

Romans 5: 9

Much more then, being now justified by his blood, we shall be saved from wrath through him.

Genesis 12: 2

And I will make of thee a great nation, and I will bless thee, and make thy name great; and thou shalt be a blessing.

A Living Hope

Today I speak over my life and over my household that God covers us in the shadow of His wings.

He who has opened this door of opportunity for me will grant me the wisdom to maximize and take full advantage of it. I am a performer and not a spectator in life. I was created a success. Things work for me. I am strong in the Lord and in the power of His might. I increase in all I do. I advance in every area of my life. My tomorrow is better than my yesterday. I have a living hope. My future is secured. Favour follows me. I am a wise person. I see my way through the challenges of life. I walk in light. Darkness is dispelled. I am jet-propelled into purpose. God did not create me as a failure. I give success its meaning. I have *good* success. My ways are pleasing unto God, and I exhibit great faith. It is my season of divine manifestation.

People will answer to me when I call. Wealth flows in my direction naturally. I cannot fail; I will not fall, I soar with wings like the eagle. I am established as praise in the earth. I am alive to the responsibilities of divine greatness inherent in me. My place in Gods divine order is sure. I go forward. I attain all that is written concerning me in the volume of the book. Mediocrity gives way to prominence, I am exalted, and my head is lifted in the midst of my peers. My rod buds! Many are called; I lead the chosen few. I have the Spirit of Counsel. I am led by the Spirit into all truth. I will not lose. I am a winner. I win always, in Jesus name. I believe and I say amen.

SELECTED AFFIRMATIONS

I am alive to the responsibilities of divine greatness inherent in me.

He who has opened this door of opportunity for me will grant me the wisdom to maximize and take full advantage of it.

1 Corinthians 16: 9

For a great door and effectual is opened unto me, and there are many adversaries.

Ephesians 6: 10

Finally, my brethren, be strong in the Lord, and in the power of his might.

1 Peter 1: 3

Blessed be the God and Father of our Lord Jesus Christ, which according to his abundant mercy hath begotten us again unto a lively hope by the resurrection of Jesus Christ from the dead.

Isaiah 40: 31

But they that wait upon the LORD shall renew their strength; they shall mount up with wings as eagles; they shall run, and not be weary; and they shall walk, and not faint.

John 16: 13

Howbeit when he, the Spirit of truth, is come, he will guide you into all truth: for he shall not speak of himself; but whatsoever he shall hear, that shall he speak: and he will shew you things to come.

No Limits

Today I speak over my life and my household that the eternal peace of the mighty God rests upon us, to keep us in safety. I insist that God will arise to my cause and aid me in all my pursuits. I am not alone, I am not forsaken, I will not be distressed, and I can do all things through Christ who strengthens me.

I am born on purpose. I will reach the point of distinction. I am set aside as a wonder to many; I have become a sign to my generation. Light from God floods my path. I have wisdom for dominion; I march on powerfully to the zone of fulfilment. I break through every wall of opposition; I overcome every obstacle; I destroy every force of limitation. I extend to the south from the north. I am jet-propelled into the fullness of Gods agenda for my life.

I am the child of the King; I have the power to rise to the top. I am seated with Christ in the heavenly places. I am above only and not beneath. I have all it takes; I excel in life. Good things happen to me. Life takes on new meaning: I am the chosen of the Lord, extremely favoured. I live in the realm of possibilities. Greatness is attracted to me. I defy failure. I rise above the heights and all the odds stacked against me. I am victorious, in Jesus name. I believe and I say amen.

SELECTED AFFIRMATIONS

I insist that God will arise to my cause and aid me in all my pursuits.

I break through every wall of opposition; I overcome every obstacle; I destroy every force of limitation.

Philippians 4: 7

And the peace of God, which passeth all understanding, shall keep your hearts and minds through Christ Jesus.

Philippians 4: 13

I can do all things through Christ which strengtheneth me.

Psalm 119: 105

Thy word is a lamp unto my feet, and a light unto my path.

Ephesians 2: 6

And hath raised us up together, and made us sit together in heavenly places in Christ Jesus.

Deuteronomy 28: 13

And the LORD shall make thee the head, and not the tail; and thou shalt be above only, and thou shalt not be beneath; if that thou hearken unto the commandments of the LORD thy God, which I command thee this day, to observe and to do them.

Posterity Protected

Today I speak over my life and over my household that God will amaze us with pleasant surprises of favour and divine release of His goodness. Difficulties, struggles, and hardships bow to the might of the Holy One at work inside me. I am cocooned in the love of God and in the power of His Spirit.

I enjoy the fullness of divine mercy because I am justified; grace is abundantly bestowed on me. I am vindicated in the presence of my accusers. God is on my side; I will not be moved. My gaze is fixed on Him; I will not see shame. I have been delivered, and no evil shall come near me or my family. My children are protected. No evil eye shall see them; no evil hands shall touch them. Gods promises over them are sure. They will not be slaves in the land. They will not fall to the influence of negative peer pressure. They will rise to the top, fulfilling destiny and attaining great purpose. My children remain in health and grow in Spirit, stature, and wisdom. The angel of God watches over them. The eyes of God will be on them. I shall not weep over any of my children. I shall not bury any child. They will live and not die.

They will exceed all my positive expectations. In their days, they will arise and call me blessed. They will come to the knowledge and saving grace of the Lord and never depart from Him. They shall be strong in the Lord and in the power of His might. They are sources of joy and encouragement. I will see and experience the validation of Gods right hand in their lives, in Jesus name. I believe and I say amen.

SELECTED AFFIRMATIONS

My children remain in health and grow in Spirit, stature, and wisdom. The angel of God watches over them.

Difficulties, struggles, and hardships bow to the might of the Holy One at work inside me.

Acts 3: 10

And they knew that it was he which sat for alms at the Beautiful gate of the temple: and they were filled with wonder and amazement at that which had happened unto him.

Romans 5: 1

Therefore being justified by faith, we have peace with God through our Lord Jesus Christ.

Psalm 16: 8

I have set the LORD always before me: because he is at my right hand, I shall not be moved.

Luke 2: 52

And Jesus increased in wisdom and stature, and in favour with God and man.

Psalm 118: 17

I shall not die, but live, and declare the works of the LORD.

Luke 1: 48

For he hath regarded the low estate of his handmaiden: for, behold, from henceforth all generations shall call me blessed.

Heavenly Support

Today, I speak over my life and my household that God is the strength of our lives and our portion forever. He sustains, keeps, and guides me. I am neither forgotten nor forsaken. God is my ever-present help in the time of trouble and the day of need.

He is my keeper, He is my guard, and He is my strong tower and my shield. No evil shall come near my house; I dwell in peace eternally. God is my protection and my provision. The works of my hands are blessed, and I see increase all around me. I will not lack, and I shall not be in want; God is my source, and I have full support of heaven in all my endeavours. My eyes have seen the goodness of God in the land of the living. I march on victorious, for no weapon fashioned or formed against me prospers.

God leads me on the paths of righteousness for His names sake. I have a future and a living hope. My tomorrow is secure because God is my defence. I am strengthened with the spirit of might in my inner man. I can do all things through Christ who strengthens me. I go forward and experience divine progression in every area of my life. My borders are enlarged. My tent pegs are extended, my coasts are widened, mercy meets me, joy accompanies me, and His goodness comes with me. I am established in His love, I abide in His presence, and I have fullness of joy. He is my peace, and His love has set me free. His light shines upon me. He fights all my battles; He conquered the enemy of my soul. Nothing is impossible for me. I win all the time, in Jesus name. I believe and I say amen.

Selected Affirmations

God is my protection and my provision. The works of my hands are blessed, and I see increase all around me. I will not lack, and I shall not be in want. God is my source, and I have full support of heaven in all my endeavours.

Psalm 27: 1

The LORD is my light and my salvation; whom shall I fear? the LORD is the strength of my life; of whom shall I be afraid?

Psalm 37: 25

I have been young, and now am old; yet have I not seen the righteous forsaken, nor his seed begging bread.

Genesis 26: 13

And the man waxed great, and went forward, and grew until he became very great.

Ephesians 3: 16

That he would grant you, according to the riches of his glory, to be strengthened with might by his Spirit in the inner man.

Psalm 23: 3

He restoreth my soul: he leadeth me in the paths of righteousness for his names sake.

Abounding Grace

Today I speak over my life and over my household that God will not withhold good from us. He abounds to me in grace and lifts my head above those of my peers. My life is in His hands, and I shall not be disappointed. God will not turn me back, neither will He forsake me. I have answers to all my prayers, and God has heard me when I called Him. His ears are forever open to my cry, and His hands are upon me for good.

My mouth will yet praise His name and not be silent. I am surrounded with His favour as with a shield. I will rejoice because God is good to me, He has forgiven all my transgression and commanded His loving kindness towards me. God has shown me mercy in the land of the living; the power of His Blood has delivered me. No good thing shall He withhold from me for His righteousness sake. I am protected, and my future is sure. God will fulfil all His promises to me. I dwell in His presence forever and I never return empty. My harvest is great. My vats shall be filled; I will eat the good of the land as He fills my mouth with plenty.

Wisdom is attracted to me; lack is swallowed up in the abundance of His presence. His grace and fullness are commended to me. I retain the favour of the Lord. I lose nothing. I enter into my season of divine restoration. I have the blessing of dominion. I am blessed by the Father, in Jesus name. I believe and I say amen.

SELECTED AFFIRMATIONS

I am surrounded with His favour as with a shield.

Wisdom is attracted to me; lack is swallowed up in the abundance of His presence.

Psalm 45: 7

Thou lovest righteousness, and hatest wickedness: therefore God, thy God, hath anointed thee with the oil of gladness above thy fellows.

Psalm 109: 30

I will greatly praise the LORD with my mouth; yea, I will praise him among the multitude.

Psalm 51: 1

Have mercy upon me, O God, according to thy lovingkindness: according unto the multitude of thy tender mercies blot out my transgressions.

Psalm 27: 4

One *thing* have I desired of the LORD, that will I seek after; that I may dwell in the house of the LORD all the days of my life, to behold the beauty of the LORD, and to enquire in his temple.

Joel 2: 25

And I will restore to you the years that the locust hath eaten, the cankerworm, and the caterpillar, and the palmerworm, my great army which I sent among you.

My Secret Place

Today, I speak over my life and my household that God has destroyed every form of conspiracy of the enemy over our lives; I will not be caught in the snare of the fowler.

God will keep me in perfect peace, because my gaze is on Him. I am protected from every evil of this age. God is the strength of my right hand, He is my salvation, He is my light, and He is the strength of my life. I am kept safely in the secret place of the Most High; I am hid in Christ and in God. I dwell securely in the place where the enemy cannot penetrate, where no evil hands can touch me and no evil eyes can see me. God is my shield and my exceeding great reward. My mind is at rest in Him. Nothing moves or destabilizes me. My faith is established on the power of the Blood and the faithfulness of my Lord, my Christ and King. Im set upon the rock; I will not sink.

My destiny is real. I am born for purpose. I win always. Everything is new for my sake; God is at work in my life. I am created to succeed, I was born to excel, and I am blessed to be a blessing. I am a partaker of the divine nature. I am lifted, I go forward, I increase on all sides; I prosper, I continue to prosper till I become very prosperous, and I am upheld by the righteous right hand of the Lord. Grace is released to me. I walk into divine limitlessness. He is the Shepherd of my soul. He is in full control. He is my fortress. He is my God! He is my hope: I will make it, I will not fail, I will not fall, I will fulfil purpose, and I will exceed every expectation. I am blessed because God is on my side. Nothing can move me because I am hid in Him, in Jesus name. I believe and I say amen.

Selected Affirmations

I am hid in Christ and in God. I dwell securely in the place where the enemy cannot penetrate, where no evil hands can touch me and no evil eyes can see me.

Colossians 3: 3

For ye are dead, and your life is hid with Christ in God.

Psalm 91: 3

Surely he shall deliver thee from the snare of the fowler, and from the noisome pestilence.

Isaiah 26: 3

Thou wilt keep him in perfect peace, whose mind is stayed on thee: because he trusteth in thee.

Psalm 27: 1

The LORD is my light and my salvation; whom shall I fear? the LORD is the strength of my life; of whom shall I be afraid?

Isaiah 43: 19

Behold, I will do a new thing; now it shall spring forth; shall ye not know it? I will even make a way in the wilderness, and rivers in the desert.

Divine Security

Today I speak over my life and over my household that God has been merciful to us and will continue to show us His unfailing kindness. He will show me His faithfulness and keep me from harm at all times. God will protect me in my going out and coming in.

I hide myself and my family in the secret place of the Most High; so we can abide under the shadow of the Almighty. I insist that God is my refuge and fortress, for the remaining days of my life. God leads me by the power of His Spirit; I will not be involved in any accident whatsoever. I will not fall or be an unfortunate victim of crash or disaster. I take an insurance policy for myself and family in the eternal Blood of the everlasting covenant and secure our well-being and protection from any incursion of the enemy and destruction, in Jesus name. I turn back any attack of the enemy set against any member of my family from colleagues at work or school, friends, and acquaintances.

I will not mourn the death of anyone, and my life is secured too. I close the gate of the grave and decree life over all in my circle of influence. We shall not die! I rebuke sudden death! I speak health. I will fulfil destiny; my steps to greatness are sure, and my feet will not slip. I will stop at nothing till I become all that God purposes me to be. I defeat all enemies round about. He is my fortress. He is my God, in Jesus name. I believe and I say amen.

SELECTED AFFIRMATIONS

I take an insurance policy for myself and family in the eternal Blood of the everlasting covenant and secure our well-being and protection from any incursion of the enemy and destruction, in Jesus name.

Revelation 12: 11

And they overcame him by the blood of the Lamb, and by the word of their testimony; and they loved not their lives unto the death.

Psalm 91: 12

He that dwelleth in the secret place of the most High shall abide under the shadow of the Almighty. I will say of the LORD, He is my refuge and my fortress: my God; in him will I trust.

Psalm 118: 17

I shall not die, but live, and declare the works of the LORD.

Psalm 18: 36

Thou hast enlarged my steps under me, that my feet did not slip.

Psalm 18: 2

The LORD is my rock, and my fortress, and my deliverer; my God, my strength, in whom I will trust; my buckler, and the horn of my salvation, and my high tower.

Called According to Purpose

Today I speak over my life and my household that Gods eyes will jealously watch over us to keep us safe at all times. Because God is my keeper and my divine protection, I will not be touched by terror wherever I go. He preserves me.

The plague of the enemy is far from me, and I will not fall victim to the destruction that wastes at noon. The sun shall not smite me by day nor the moon by night. My eyes are shielded from every evil around me. God is my defence, my buckler and strong tower, my hiding place in the time of trouble. He is faithful; He will not leave or forsake me. God arises on my behalf, my enemies are scattered, and those who rise against me melt like wax before the fire of God. I am hid from all the danger that destroys in this age; because I am called according to purpose, everything is working for me.

I am loved by God. He loved me first, and God is at work in me both to will and do of His good pleasure. I have peace; my ways are pleasing unto God. My enemies are at peace with me. I am secure on all sides; in Him I overcome. My faith rises to another level in the midst of difficulties. This too shall pass, like every other one before it. I rise with wings as an eagle. I escape unhurt. I am an overcomer. Stones dont stop me. I am strong in the Lord and in the power of His might. I achieve greatness as destined. Eternity is in focus. I cant be derailed. My destiny is sure. I am a prophetic ambassador. Now is my time. I shine like the light, in Jesus name. I believe and I say amen.

SELECTED AFFIRMATIONS

I am hid from all the danger that destroys in this age; because I am the called according to purpose, everything is working for me.

Romans 8: 28

And we know that all things work together for good to them that love God, to them who are the called according to his purpose.

Psalm 91: 10

There shall no evil befall thee, neither shall any plague come nigh thy dwelling.

Psalm 91: 4

He shall cover thee with his feathers, and under his wings shalt thou trust: his truth shall be thy shield and buckler.

Proverbs 16: 7

When a mans ways please the Lord, he maketh even his enemies to be at peace with him.

Isaiah 40: 31

But they that wait upon the Lord shall renew their strength; they shall mount up with wings as eagles; they shall run, and not be weary; and they shall walk, and not faint.

Created for Maximum Impact

Today I speak over my life and my household that God has lifted up our heads and let the light of His Word shine over us again.

God has remembered me for good according to His promise and shows me good in the land of the living. The power in the name and the Blood of the eternal covenant have set me in the proper place in life. Considering the finished work of Calvarys cross, the infallible Word of God, and the testimony of Jesus which is the spirit of prophecy, I invoke every blessing of God upon my life and household. I declare that I will live and not die. I am strong in the Lord. I am established as a praise in life. I will not disappear suddenly, neither will my memory perish. I wax from strength to strength; I am the righteousness of God in Christ Jesus. My destiny will not be truncated, I will not be stranded in Life, and I will fulfil purpose. My inheritance in God remains in place. The spirit of fear is defeated in my life; I rise above every intimidation of the enemy.

The lines have fallen for me in pleasant places; my heritage is goodly. My tomorrow is better than my yesterday. I have the oil of ease; nothing is difficult for me. I enter into my season of manifestation. I am an element of positive change to the world, created for maximum impact. I am a son of consolation, I am the salt of the earth, and I am the light of the world, a city set on a hill. My influence cannot be hid. I am limitless. I am an ambassador of heaven. The earth answers to me. Infirmity stays off my body; it is the temple of the Holy Spirit. I prosper in all I do, and darkness is defeated. The angels stand guard; I am protected, in Jesus name. I believe and I say amen.

Selected Affirmations

Today I speak over my life and my household that God has lifted up our heads.

Psalm 3: 3

But thou, O Lord, art a shield for me; my glory, and the lifter up of mine head.

2 Corinthians 5: 20

Now then we are ambassadors for Christ, as though God did beseech you by us: we pray you in Christs stead, be ye reconciled to God.

1 Chronicles 11: 9

So David waxed greater and greater: for the Lord of hosts was with him.

Psalm 16: 6

The lines are fallen unto me in pleasant places; yea, I have a goodly heritage.

Psalm 1: 3

And he shall be like a tree planted by the rivers of water, that bringeth forth his fruit in his season; his leaf also shall not wither; and whatsoever he doeth shall prosper.

Lasting Testimony

Today I speak over my life and my household that God is for us an ever-increasing weight of glory. He will show Himself strong on my behalf as He vindicates me. He lifts my head in the midst of my peers and announces my victory in the camp of my foes.

My enemies are beaten down completely round about me, and their remembrance vanishes. Their heads are buried in shame, but I will not be disgraced. God has enlarged my coast, and He has increased my renown. He has issued the decree and set me above all those who hate me. I have been promoted, and all eyes will see the exaltation of the Lord in my life. It is the start of something new, it is the beginning of a new chapter, and my encounter with the Lord leaves me with a lasting testimony. I will only go forward from here.

I increase on all sides. I walk into divine favour everywhere I go. The Spirit of the Lord seals my testimony. I am set free by the power of the Lord. God is my banner of righteousness: I am protected in His love; I am forgiven by His grace. I have received mercy because of His kindness; He is faithful to me. I am a sign and wonder to my generation. I have been lifted; my shoulder has been relieved of the heavy load, the yoke is shattered, and the burden is destroyed. I am anointed to become all I was created to be. Good success is attracted to me. Wealth and goodness accompany me on my journey. I will run and not be ruined. I will end well. I will exceed every expectation, in Jesus name. I believe and I say amen.

SELECTED AFFIRMATIONS

God has enlarged my coast, and He has increased my renown.

Isaiah 54: 2

Enlarge the place of thy tent, and let them stretch forth the curtains of thine habitations: spare not, lengthen thy cords, and strengthen thy stakes.

Psalm 23: 6

Surely goodness and mercy shall follow me all the days of my life: and I will dwell in the house of the LORD for ever.

Psalm 71: 21

Thou shalt increase my greatness, and comfort me on every side.

Isaiah 8: 18

Behold, I and the children whom the LORD hath given me are for signs and for wonders in Israel from the LORD of hosts, which dwelleth in mount Zion.

Isaiah 10: 27

And it shall come to pass in that day, that his burden shall be taken away from off thy shoulder, and his yoke from off thy neck, and the yoke shall be destroyed because of the anointing.

Angelic Support

Today I speak over my life and my household that God has separated us for the blessing, thus causing my rod to bud. I have angelic support and divine enablement; the Spirit of God gives me the grace. I overcome every power of the enemy; the dew of heaven brings me refreshing.

Gods glory is revealed in my life. I enter into the pavilion of the Almighty by the Blood of the Lamb. I am safe, I lay hold of the horns of the altar, and the avenger of death cannot fall upon me. I am established on the heights of God, far from every lie of the enemy; my head is anointed afresh, I am empowered to conquer, I break through on all sides, and my sun will not set at noon. I am appointed for promotion, and I am blessed beyond the curse. I cannot be stopped; I have divine acceleration, and the sower overtakes the reaper. I have divine open doors; time and chance happen to me for good.

My word has found me out: I am unfettered to run, my race is unhindered, and the top is my destination. I have life eternal, I have life abundant, I have the life of God in me. I move into the realms of the extraordinary and am established there. I ride on the wings of eagles; I am not weary, and I will not faint. I am a positive change agent. I am a voice in my generation. Good things happen to me, in Jesus name. I believe and I say amen.

Selected Affirmations

I am established on the heights of God, far from every lie of the enemy; my head is anointed afresh.

Psalm 92: 10

But my horn shalt thou exalt like the horn of an unicorn: I shall be anointed with fresh oil.

Numbers 17: 8

And it came to pass, that on the morrow Moses went into the tabernacle of witness; and, behold, the rod of Aaron for the house of Levi was budded, and brought forth buds, and bloomed blossoms, and yielded almonds.

Psalm 27: 5

For in the time of trouble he shall hide me in his pavilion: in the secret of his tabernacle shall he hide me; he shall set me up upon a rock.

Isaiah 40: 31

But they that wait upon the Lord shall renew their strength; they shall mount up with wings as eagles; they shall run, and not be weary; and they shall walk, and not faint.

Amos 9: 13

Behold, the days come, saith the Lord, that the ploughman shall overtake the reaper, and the treader of grapes him that soweth seed; and the mountains shall drop sweet wine, and all the hills shall melt.

Blessed to Bless

Today I speak over my life and over my household that God will increase our revelational knowledge of Him and show us His glory every day of our lives.

God will show me His goodness in the land of the living and magnify my lot in life. I am mighty in the land, and my mouth will feast on the fat of it. I have grain in excess, milk in abundance and wine in plenty. My storehouse is full of Gods bounty; I have no lack. My vat overflows. I am in the realm of possibilities. I am favoured beyond every limitation. Grace and mercy are my portion. I am the righteousness of God in Christ Jesus. The edge around me remains unbroken; I am kept, I am protected. Angels do my bidding, Gods ears are turned in my direction, and I have answers to my prayers, speedy response to my requests. I walk in confidence; all things are working for me. I am the blessing of God, blessed to be a blessing.

My generation will feel the impact of my sojourn; I am an addition to value. I am a child of consolation, a son of encouragement. I exceed all expectations. I have joy unspeakable; I am totally unstoppable. Everything I lay my hands on succeeds. God has comforted me on all sides, and He has increased my greatness. I go forward and I am lifted. I am seated in heavenly places, my destiny is secured in Him; purpose has found me, I cannot be stranded. I am complete in Him. I lack nothing; I live in sufficiency. He is my shepherd; I shall not want. I am planted in the fullness of His household, and heaven supports me, in Jesus name. I believe and I say amen.

Selected Affirmations

God has comforted me on all sides, and He has increased my greatness.

Psalm 71: 21

Thou shalt increase my greatness, and comfort me on every side.

Proverbs 3: 10

So shall thy barns be filled with plenty, and thy presses shall burst out with new wine.

Psalm 23: 1

The LORD is my shepherd; I shall not want.

Psalm 1: 3

And he shall be like a tree planted by the rivers of water, that bringeth forth his fruit in his season; his leaf also shall not wither; and whatsoever he doeth shall prosper.

Psalm 92: 13

Those that be planted in the house of the LORD shall flourish in the courts of our God.

Redeemed Soul

Today I speak over my life and my household that God has granted us unfettered access into His presence. I have joy unspeakable, full of glory. The power of the pleasure available at His right hand destroys the yoke of pressure upon my life.

I affirm that His body was broken for me and His blood was shed on the cross, so by His stripes I am healed, and my sins are forgiven. My soul is redeemed; my life is in His hands. My future is bright. Im the apple of His eye; I am protected, and the works of my hands are established. No evil shall come near my hiding. I have perfect peace because I have put my trust in Him. He is the shepherd of my soul; I hear His voice as He leads me on the paths of righteousness for His names sake.

I am free indeed because the Lord has set me free. The yoke is broken and the burden is destroyed by the reason of the anointing oil; my shoulder is relieved of every heavy basket. I am destined for the top; my life is a pleasant flow of greatness from His court. I am delivered from every form of corruption; I shine like light, and I prosper in all I do. I am limitless by nature; I increase every day. I have received mercy, I am blessed by God, and I am a blessing. I am created for dominion. I will not fail or fall but will fulfil purpose and exceed every expectation. I am blessed with God on my side. Nothing can move me, in Jesus name. I believe and I say amen.

Selected Affirmations

I am free indeed because the Lord has set me free. The yoke is broken and the burden is destroyed by the reason of the anointing oil; my life is a pleasant flow of greatness from His court.

Isaiah 10: 27

And it shall come to pass in that day, that his burden shall be taken away from off thy shoulder, and his yoke from off thy neck, and the yoke shall be destroyed because of the anointing.

Genesis 12: 2

And I will make of thee a great nation, and I will bless thee, and make thy name great; and thou shalt be a blessing.

Isaiah 53: 5

But he was wounded for our transgressions, he was bruised for our iniquities: the chastisement of our peace was upon him; and with his stripes we are healed.

Psalm 16: 10

For thou wilt not leave my soul in hell; neither wilt thou suffer thine Holy One to see corruption.

Psalm 8: 6

Thou madest him to have dominion over the works of thy hands; thou hast put all things under his feet.

Brand New

Today I speak over my life and my household that God has turned our situations and circumstances around for the better. I experience His power afresh, and so I receive the grace to will and do of His good pleasure in all things and at all times.

The days of affliction are over; my change is here. My captivity is turned around, my broken dreams are mended, and I have a brand-new start. He makes all things brand-new. Life eternal flows into me; abundant life is my portion; I run not in vain, I call Him not in vain; all my requests are granted. God is for me, and nothing is against me. I run through a troop. I leap over a wall. I am defended in battle; He is the covering for my head in the fight. He is mighty to save; He has taken away my shame and preserved me from destruction. God rejoices over me with singing and song; my hands are lifted in triumph over my enemies, and all my foes have been destroyed. I stand strong in the Lord and in the power of His might. My life is hid in Christ and in God, and no harm can befall me!

Many will seek my good; favour surrounds me as a shield. My faith stands strong. I am blessed beyond the curse. I am created and empowered for the top. I remain a city on a hill, and my impact is global. I am eternally relevant to Gods scheme of things; my glory cannot be covered. The tops of my mountains are visible for all eyes to see. I will not be passed on by events. I remain on the cutting edge in my generation. God loves me, in Jesus name. I believe and I say amen.

Selected Affirmations

The days of affliction are over; my change is here. My captivity is turned around; my broken dreams are mended.

Psalm 126: 1

When the LORD turned again the captivity of Zion, we were like them that dream.

Jeremiah 29: 11

For I know the thoughts that I think toward you, saith the LORD, thoughts of peace, and not of evil, to give you an expected end.

Philippians 2: 13

For it is God which worketh in you both to will and to do of his good pleasure.

Galatians 3: 13

Christ hath redeemed us from the curse of the law, being made a curse for us: for it is written, Cursed is every one that hangeth on a tree.

Psalm 5: 12

For thou, LORD, wilt bless the righteous; with favour wilt thou compass him as with a shield.

No Weight in the Wait

Today I speak over my life and my household that God will neither forget nor forsake us. He will remember me for good and deliver on all His promises to me. All that God has spoken concerning me comes to pass.

My times and seasons have changed. The mercy of the Lord my God has found me; I rejoice in the Lord for the fulfilment of all His promises to me. Weeping in the night season ends! Joy is here, and a new day dawns! It is morning; my path is flooded with light. Surely there is an end to frustration, darkness, and confusion; the expectations of my heart are fulfilled. I am not disappointed, and I have not been disgraced! God is faithful to me. He took the weight out of my wait; my change has come, mourning gives way to dancing, sackcloth gives way to the garments of joy, and beauty has replaced ashes. My tongue praises the Lord! Nothing can shut my gates of praise; no one can pull down my hands raised in worship. My glory will yet praise His name and not be silent.

God is marvellous to me. The sun shines for me, the Sun of Righteousness arises on my behalf with healing in His wings, and no part of my life is spared the force of its impact. My body is healed; my soul is saved, my heart is mended, my finances are restored, my relationships are sorted, and my eternity is secure. I am a blessed person and a blessing unto many. He leads me in the way I should go. I profit wherever I turn to. Doors open up to me, and I have a good heritage. I am established in His presence. I rejoice in the power of His love. I emerge as a force to be reckoned with in my days. I am the light of the world and the salt of the earth, in Jesus name. I believe and I say amen.

SELECTED AFFIRMATIONS

I speak over my life and my household that God will neither forget nor forsake us.

1 Kings 8: 57

The LORD our God be with us, as he was with our fathers: let him not leave us, nor forsake us.

Psalm 30: 11

Thou hast turned for me my mourning into dancing: thou hast put off my sackcloth, and girded me with gladness.

Psalm 30: 5

For his anger endureth but a moment; in his favour is life: weeping may endure for a night, but joy cometh in the morning.

Malachi 4: 2

But unto you that fear my name shall the Sun of righteousness arise with healing in his wings; and ye shall go forth, and grow up as calves of the stall.

Matthew 5: 14

Ye are the light of the world. A city that is set on an hill cannot be hid.

My Shepherd

Today I speak over my life and my household that God is for us. He watches over me through every situation and in every circumstance. When I walk through the fire, it will not scorch me; neither will its flames kindle upon me. When I go through the water, it will not over flow me neither will I drown in it. Even if I walk through the valley of the shadow of death, I will fear no evil; because God is with me; I am comforted by His rod and His staff.

I am satisfied with the joy of His presence; I have joy unspeakable, full of glory. I have eternal pleasures, and He will neither leave nor forsake me. I am kept from evil, and no harm befalls me. I am hid in the shadow of His wings; I find refuge in the courts of my King, and nothing will come near me. I have authority to trample on snakes and scorpions and to overcome all the powers of the enemy; nothing will harm me. He that keeps me neither sleeps nor slumbers; I remain eternally safe and secure. No terror shall come near me by day, nor the destruction by night, nor the arrow that wastes by noontime. I am guarded and protected by an innumerable company of angels.

My future is hid in God, my destiny is secure, and my posterity is protected. God is my keeper and the strength of my life. Fear is banished; inhibitions are destroyed. God is my help. He will watch over me and turn back every ill will of the enemy. I am confident in the power of His mercy and love for me. He is my fortress; I will never be shaken. My hope and trust are in God, my Maker. My faith in Him overcomes the world. I am victorious because God is with me, in Jesus name. I believe and I say amen.

Selected Affirmations

My future is hid in God, my destiny is secure and my posterity is protected. God is my keeper and the strength of my life.

Psalm 121: 5

The Lord is thy keeper: the Lord is thy shade upon thy right hand.

Psalm 91: 1

He that dwelleth in the secret place of the most High shall abide under the shadow of the Almighty.

Luke 10: 19

Behold, I give unto you power to tread on serpents and scorpions, and over all the power of the enemy: and nothing shall by any means hurt you.

Hebrews 12: 22

But ye are come unto mount Sion, and unto the city of the living God, the heavenly Jerusalem, and to an innumerable company of angels.

1 John 5: 4

For whatsoever is born of God overcometh the world: and this is the victory that overcometh the world, even our faith.

Delivered from Infirmity

Today I speak over my life and over my household that the finished work of the cross of Calvary has set us free from every affliction of sickness and disease.

I am free from the law and the power of sin. His body was broken, so mine is made whole; His blood was shed, so my life is secure. I will live and shall not die. I shall live out the full implication of my life. My destiny will not be truncated; I will not be cut off in the midst of my days. I shall not cast my young; rather, my seed will endure. My life is intact. By His stripes I am healed. I will not work in vain. The earth will yield of her increase to me on all fronts. The works of my hands are blessed. I shall enjoy the full benefits of salvation; my soul will prosper, and I will be in health. My life is safe and my eternity sure.

My struggle with sin is over; I have the grace of God. I live a godly life. I am assisted by the sweet Spirit of holiness. I am helped by the angels of God. Mercy, love, peace, and joy are my companions in this race of life. I shall not be stranded. I have light on my path, so I walk not in darkness. I am led by God; I am filled with His Spirit. I prosper wherever I turn; good things happen to me. I am the righteousness of God in Christ Jesus. He died so I may live; He lives in me. He is the earnest of my redemption, in Jesus name. I believe and I say amen.

SELECTED AFFIRMATIONS

The finished work of the cross of Calvary has set us free from every affliction of sickness and disease.

Galatians 5: 1

Stand fast therefore in the liberty wherewith Christ hath made us free, and be not entangled again with the yoke of bondage.

Job 42: 17

So Job died, being old and full of days.

Exodus 23: 26

There shall nothing cast their young, nor be barren, in thy land: the number of thy days I will fulfil.

Psalm 71: 21

Thou shalt increase my greatness, and comfort me on every side.

Psalm 119: 105

Thy word is a lamp unto my feet, and a light unto my path.

Standing on the Rock

Today I speak over my life and over my household that God will remember His promises to us and fulfil all His words towards me. I will not be shaken, though the mountains may be removed. I stand on the power of His word; He is the Lord my God.

I shall not fear anything; God is faithful, and I abide in Him. I trust in the Lord my God; He is the rock of my salvation and my fortress. I run into the mighty Fortress that is my God. I will not see shame. I have light by the strength of His word. In His light, I see light. Darkness is dispelled, and frustration is turned around. I have received mercy and great grace; His loving kindness has found me, and I am restored according to the goodness of His love. He has declared it, and I have it. I am healed, I am restored, I am blessed above the curse, I am lifted above all my peers, and I break through on all sides. I rise above every element of containment. I have dominion. I multiply! I have peace like a river! I am above only and not beneath; the sons of the stranger shall serve me. I am promoted by the God who dwells in Zion; I am for signs and wonders! I press on to the saving of my soul. I prosper always, my tomorrow is better than my yesterday.

I have a blessed life. I am a fruitful vine; I am victorious in Him. I live and have eternal life in me. Nothing is impossible for me. I am loved by many and accepted in the Beloved. Blessed are those who bless me. His promises are mine, in Jesus, name. I believe and I say amen.

Selected Affirmations

I will not be shaken, though the mountains may be removed. I stand on the power of His word; He is the Lord my God.

Psalm 61: 2

From the end of the earth will I cry unto thee, when my heart is overwhelmed: lead me to the rock that is higher than I.

Psalm 71: 3

Be thou my strong habitation, whereunto I may continually resort: thou hast given commandment to save me; for thou art my rock and my fortress.

Luke 1: 37

For with God nothing shall be impossible.

Isaiah 54: 3

For thou shalt break forth on the right hand and on the left; and thy seed shall inherit the Gentiles, and make the desolate cities to be inhabited.

Ephesians 1: 6

To the praise of the glory of his grace, wherein he hath made us accepted in the beloved.

Divine Validation

Today I speak over my life and over my household that God will turn His ears to our cry. He will neither deny nor forsake me in the day of trouble. I am helped by God in every one of lifes situation and circumstances.

My plea for mercy will not go unheeded. God is with me, through the fire and through the flood. I am not alone; God is involved in my life. My battle is the Lords: I hold my peace, and He fights for me. God hears my supplication, and my prayers are answered. I come to the God of all the universe, and I will not return empty; all my requests are granted, and I have responses to all my calls in prayer. God answers me according to the faithfulness of His name. I am strengthened, hope is renewed, I can see tomorrow, and grace is restored. The power of the Lord is available to assist me. I plug into His goodness. I find grace to help in the time of need. God is my keeper; I am a watered garden, I bring out my fruit in season, my roots are strong in the ground, and I have life. My rod buds. I am eternally assisted; I am empowered by the Spirit of the living God. I am refreshed by the dew of heaven. I have light; I shine brightly in the darkness. My light endures.

The glory of the Lord is risen upon me. I take my rightful place in the scheme of Gods plan. Purpose is revealed; destiny is attained. Glory is made manifest. Greatness is attracted. Mercy is shown. Kindness is embraced. I enter into my season of divine validation; I am encouraged by Gods faithfulness. Everything works for me; nothing is against me, in Jesus name. I believe and I say amen.

SELECTED AFFIRMATIONS

I am not alone; God is involved in my life. The power of the Lord is available to assist me.

Acts 1: 8

But ye shall receive power, after that the Holy Ghost is come upon you: and ye shall be witnesses unto me both in Jerusalem, and in all Judaea, and in Samaria, and unto the uttermost part of the earth.

Isaiah 60: 1

Arise, shine; for thy light is come, and the glory of the LORD is risen upon thee.

Romans 8: 28

And we know that all things work together for good to them that love God, to them who are the called according to his purpose.

Isaiah 40: 5

And the glory of the LORD shall be revealed, and all flesh shall see it together: for the mouth of the LORD hath spoken it.

Isaiah 58: 11

And the LORD shall guide thee continually, and satisfy thy soul in drought, and make fat thy bones: and thou shalt be like a watered garden, and like a spring of water, whose waters fail not.

The Keeping Power

Today I speak over my life and over my household that the grace of God will keep us, and the power of His Spirit will preserve us.

God is my strength and my salvation; I will not fear. Indeed He is my light and my salvation; I will not fret. I am surrounded by His angels, and nothing moves me. I trust in the keeping power of the Almighty and remain confident in the everlasting love of the King of glory. I am loved with an everlasting love. God has me covered. Though a thousand shall fall at my side and ten thousand at my right hand, I shall not fear; God watches over me and mine. He that keeps me neither sleeps nor slumbers. The Lord remembers His promises and fulfils His covenant to me. My life is safe, and my future is not under threat.

I exceed all expectations, I deliver on destinys terms; I operate in the arena of limitless possibilities, I have become a wonder to many, and God is my sustenance. He is my eternal help and source. I shall not want. My mouth is satisfied with good things, I will eat of the fat of the land; I am like a tree planted by the rivers of flowing water, my root is strong in the ground. My leaves are green and fresh. I bring forth my fruit in and out of season. The earth will yield to me of her increase. I am numbered among the mighty, I have a part with the strong. I am ordained a success. I am Heaven assisted, I am angels protected; I am divinely empowered, and spiritually enabled for global prominence. I come into my season of divine recognition, in Jesus name. I believe and I say amen.

SELECTED AFFIRMATIONS

I trust in the keeping power of the Almighty and remain confident in the everlasting love of the King of glory.

Jeremiah 31: 3

The LORD hath appeared of old unto me, saying, Yea, I have loved thee with an everlasting love: therefore with lovingkindness have I drawn thee.

Psalm 27: 1

The LORD is my light and my salvation; whom shall I fear? the LORD is the strength of my life; of whom shall I be afraid?

Psalm 91: 7

A thousand shall fall at thy side, and ten thousand at thy right hand; but it shall not come nigh thee.

Ephesians 3: 20

Now unto him that is able to do exceeding abundantly above all that we ask or think, according to the power that worketh in us.

Psalm 67: 6

Then shall the earth yield her increase; and God, even our own God, shall bless us.

Illuminated Paths

Today I speak over my life and my household that the mercy of God will separate us for good. God is good to me, and I have received His compassion. My paths are illuminated, and I walk in the light of His Word.

I walk into the enlarged place; I am directed by the eyes of the Lord. I enter into the wealthy place; things have turned around for me. I have been redeemed by the mercy of the Lord; I have newness of life. I am ushered into greatness; I am loved of God. I am called according to purpose. I am protected by the power of His love; He is my glory and the lifter of my head. My head is covered in the midst of the battle; my gaze is on Him, and I will not see shame. I put my trust in Him at all times, and I will not be destroyed. I am hid in the safety of His tabernacle, provided for in the abundance of His household. I am not forsaken; I am the apple of His eye, and I am forgiven.

I have been restored to greatness. My profiting is sure; I have been empowered to get wealth. I am the righteousness of God in Christ Jesus. I am established in love. I have all it takes to be the best in life. I am lifted above all my enemies because I have been chosen by God. I move unto better things as revealed in the promises of God. It is the start of a new season. Its a new day. Nothing limits me. Nothing can stop me, in Jesus name. I believe and I say amen.

SELECTED AFFIRMATIONS

I walk in the light of His Word. I walk into the enlarged place; I am directed by the eyes of the Lord.

Psalm 119: 105

Thy word is a lamp unto my feet, and a light unto my path.

Psalm 66: 12

Thou hast caused men to ride over our heads; we went through fire and through water: but thou broughtest us out into a wealthy place.

Proverbs 3: 10

So shall thy barns be filled with plenty, and thy presses shall burst out with new wine.

Deuteronomy 8: 18

But thou shalt remember the LORD thy God: for it is he that giveth thee power to get wealth, that he may establish his covenant which he sware unto thy fathers, as it is this day.

Psalm 27: 6

And now shall mine head be lifted up above mine enemies round about me: therefore will I offer in his tabernacle sacrifices of joy; I will sing, yea, I will sing praises unto the LORD.

Unusually Favoured

Today I speak over my life and my household that every plan and purpose of God concerning us will be fulfilled. I find full expression in God; nothing is impossible for me. I have the oil of ease, and nothing is difficult for me.

I operate with wisdom. I see my way through every difficult terrain. I will not be held back or limited by the force of frustration. I move with the revelation of the mind of Christ. Doors open up to me at will; I break through on all fronts and on every side. Greatness is attracted to me; success is attached to all I do. I prosper supernaturally. I dwell in light; darkness has no hold or power over me. I am created for dominion; I rise to the top in every situation. I am gifted and prepared as a solution provider. My inheritance in God remains unaltered. Of my rise there is no end; concerning my progress, there is no limit; about my status, I excel.

I am the zenith of Gods creation; I manifest the good works of God in Christ Jesus. I walk tall through the issues of life. His thoughts of good and not of evil deliver to me a bright future; I have a living hope according to His divine plan. Everything works for the purpose of His will. I am helped by God. Nothing is lost. I live on the island of divine restoration as He has instructed. I get more than I bargain for; I dwell in unusual favour, people will honour me, and I will be promoted. I see good and experience Gods grace at all times because I was created in His image and likeness. Its all according to His plan, in Jesus name. I believe and I say amen.

Selected Affirmations

I will not be held back or limited by the force of frustration. I move with the revelation of the mind of Christ. Doors open up to me at will. I break through on all fronts and on every side.

1 Corinthians 2: 16

For who hath known the mind of the Lord, that he may instruct him? but we have the mind of Christ.

Ephesians 2: 10

For we are his workmanship, created in Christ Jesus unto good works, which God hath before ordained that we should walk in them.

Romans 8: 28

And we know that all things work together for good to them that love God, to them who are the called according to his purpose.

Mark 10: 27

And Jesus looking upon them saith, With men it is impossible, but not with God: for with God all things are possible.

2 Corinthians 12: 9

And he said unto me, My grace is sufficient for thee: for my strength is made perfect in weakness. Most gladly therefore will I rather glory in my infirmities, that the power of Christ may rest upon me.

Due for Elevation

Today I speak over my life and my household that God will show Himself faithful on our behalf and support our cause.

God is my help in every situation. He is my strength in times of weariness and my banner in the time of war. God is my defence; I am completely covered by His everlasting arms of love and His solace for me through the trials of life. I have comfort through the season of pain. I am not deserted, I am not abandoned, and I am not forsaken; my times and seasons are in His hands. I am due for elevation. He commands change, and my season changes. I am lifted, I am favoured; He leads me on the paths of righteousness for His names sake. I reside in the courts of my Lord, I dwell in the presence of the King, I am accepted in the beloved, and my eyes behold the glory of the Maker of all things. He is my fortress; I will never be shaken. I put my trust in Him; I will not see shame or disgrace. God is for me, and nothing can be against me. God is before me. I have found mercy; I am comforted, I am encouraged in the Lord, and I find peace in the centre of His will.

This is my season of elevation in Christ. I have been blessed with all spiritual consecrations, and I move into the manifestation of Gods commanded blessings. The wait is over; its my time and its my season, in Jesus name. I believe and I say amen.

Selected Affirmations

He commands change, and my season changes.

Ezekiel 34: 26

And I will make them and the places round about my hill a blessing; and I will cause the shower to come down in his season; there shall be showers of blessing.

Psalm 9: 10

And they that know thy name will put their trust in thee: for thou, Lord, hast not forsaken them that seek thee.

2 Corinthians 12: 9

And he said unto me, My grace is sufficient for thee: for my strength is made perfect in weakness. Most gladly therefore will I rather glory in my infirmities, that the power of Christ may rest upon me.

Romans 8: 31

What shall we then say to these things? If God be for us, who can be against us?

Ephesians 1: 3

Blessed be the God and Father of our Lord Jesus Christ, who hath blessed us with all spiritual blessings in heavenly places in Christ.

Season of Upward Lift

Today I speak over my life and my household that God has broken every yoke of delay in every area of our lives.

Every force of limitation is destroyed in my existence; I break every chain and blast through every wall of concealment. I walk into divine opportunities on time. My steps are ordered by God. I see my way, I walk up the ladder of promotion, and I step up the stage in elevation. My season of upward lift is upon me, I am called up to greatness suddenly, and I am kept in place and established in position permanently. All eyes shall see and bless the name of my God. My name is mentioned in the corridors of power. I am seated with the nobles; Gods call to greatness is imminent. I am forever on the rise; there is no end to the extent of my elevation. My star shines, and my light shines in the darkness. I am the delight of the Lord, He watches over His word concerning me. Nothing holds me bound, and no one keeps me down. I am constantly in motion towards the mark; the prize is in view, and I will apprehend for the reason for which I have been apprehended.

My helpers will locate me. I walk and will not be weary; I run and will not be faint. The gates are open, the doors are ajar, and the windows are unlocked. I have access by the Blood of the Lamb; I have the keys of David. My storehouses are open, and every blessing from God gets to me on time. I am not delayed, and I cant be denied, in Jesus name.
I believe and I say amen.

Selected Affirmations

My name is mentioned in the corridors of power. I am seated with the nobles; Gods call to greatness is imminent.

Genesis 12: 2

And I will make of thee a great nation, and I will bless thee, and make thy name great; and thou shalt be a blessing.

1 Samuel 2: 8

He raiseth up the poor out of the dust, and lifteth up the beggar from the dunghill, to set them among princes, and to make them inherit the throne of glory: for the pillars of the earth are the Lords, and he hath set the world upon them.

Jeremiah 1: 12

Then said the Lord unto me, Thou hast well seen: for I will hasten my word to perform it.

Philippians 3: 13

Brethren, I count not myself to have apprehended: but this one thing I do, forgetting those things which are behind, and reaching forth unto those things which are before.

Isaiah 22: 22

And the key of the house of David will I lay upon his shoulder; so he shall open, and none shall shut; and he shall shut, and none shall open.

Saved to Serve

Today I speak over my life and my household that God has come quickly to our aid. He raises help for me speedily. I will not lack supernatural help; I have angelic assistance everywhere I turn to.

I walk into my blessings suddenly. My path drips with fatness; I am delivered from afflictions and trials because I am the called according to His purpose. I am led in the way to go, and He holds me by the hand. I am protected from the pit without water; I will not fall into the well without water. My life is preserved, my destiny is unhampered, and my purpose is intact. I find His love everywhere I turn. I am not stranded. He is with me. I have access to His presence by the power of His Blood; I am accepted by the Beloved. I am not condemned; I am justified, I am blessed beyond the curse, and I am the redeemed of the Lord. I have all that pertains to life and goodliness.

I am saved to serve; my service is not in vain, because he upholds me with His righteous right hand. Before I call, He will answer. Before I ask, I receive; before I seek, I find; before I knock, it is opened unto me. My walls are ever before Him. He answers my prayers and grants all my requests. I find answers to all my questions. I have the mind of Christ; I am wise with wisdom that is from above, the wisdom to fulfil purpose. Darkness will not obscure my glory; it blazes forth like light out of His presence. I see my way through. I work my way out. I have an outstanding testimony, and greatness is attracted to me. I have good success in my service, in all things and at all times. I am sought after by many; I am a solution provider, praised in my generation. God is my source, in Jesus name. I believe and I say amen.

Selected Affirmations

I am saved to serve; my service is not in vain, because he upholds me with His righteous right hand.

Isaiah 41: 10

Fear thou not; for I am with thee: be not dismayed; for I am thy God: I will strengthen thee; yea, I will help thee; yea, I will uphold thee with the right hand of my righteousness.

Ephesians 1: 1718

That the God of our Lord Jesus Christ, the Father of glory, may give unto you the spirit of wisdom and revelation in the knowledge of him: the eyes of your understanding being enlightened; that ye may know what is the hope of his calling, and what the riches of the glory of his inheritance in the saints

Ephesians 1: 6

To the praise of the glory of his grace, wherein he hath made us accepted in the beloved.

2 Peter 1: 3

According as his divine power hath given unto us all things that pertain unto life and godliness, through the knowledge of him that hath called us to glory and virtue.

Isaiah 65: 24

And it shall come to pass, that before they call, I will answer; and while they are yet speaking, I will hear.

A Glorious Future

Today I speak over my life and my household that God will amaze us with pleasant surprises from now till the end of our lives. I insist that my tomorrow is better than my yesterday; every day is an addition to the previous. I walk into a glorious future, and things have turned around for my good.

My sun will not set at noon; the brightness of my rising attracts greatness from every wing of the wind. I soar like the eagle far into the skies, away from every force of limitation. I am unhindered by the power of my past; I am delivered into the possibilities of my divine destiny. God favours me above the rest; I am lifted higher than everyone before me. Wisdom, knowledge, counsel, might, and dominion are visible in my life. I add value to creation. God sustains me; He is my resource, and I am empowered to prosper, a tremendous blessing to all whom I come in contact with. I have joy like the ceaseless flow of a river; I am glorious in the righteousness of the Lord. I go forward. I am unstoppable; I am assisted by heaven, divinely supported, and my purpose is fulfilled. God is glorified.

Everything is possible, and my faith is great. I call forth my seasons. My change is here; I am a praise in the earth. My story has changed. The heavens give rain to my seed, and I have a bountiful harvest. The works of my hands are blessed. I am victorious in battle, my strength is renewed, and my feet are strong. I march on fearlessly. I take new territories; I am established gloriously in Jesus name. I believe and I say amen.

Selected Affirmations

I soar like the eagle far into the skies, away from every force of limitation. I am unhindered by the power of my past; I am delivered into the possibilities of my divine destiny.

Philippians 3: 13

Brethren, I count not myself to have apprehended: but this one thing I do, forgetting those things which are behind, and reaching forth unto those things which are before.

Isaiah 11: 2

And the spirit of the LORD shall rest upon him, the spirit of wisdom and understanding, the spirit of counsel and might, the spirit of knowledge and of the fear of the LORD.

Psalm 85: 12

Yea, the LORD shall give that which is good; and our land shall yield her increase.

Psalm 103: 5

Who satisfieth thy mouth with good things; so that thy youth is renewed like the eagles.

Deuteronomy 8: 18

But thou shalt remember the LORD thy God: for it is he that giveth thee power to get wealth, that he may establish his covenant which he sware unto thy fathers, as it is this day.

Power over Evil

Today I speak over my life and household that God will jealously stand guard over us and permanently watch over my destiny. I am protected by the Son; my life is hid in Christ as He is hid in God. I am secure in Jesus, in heaven, far above every power of the enemy. No evil or harm will befall me.

I take refuge in the name of the Lord. I run into the strong tower, and I am safe in the arms of the Master; the spirit of fear is rebuked. I have the spirit of power, I have the spirit of might, I have a sound mind, and I manifest the wisdom of God in all that I do. I have the authority, so I trample on snakes and scorpions. I have the power to overcome all the powers of the enemy; no weapon formed or fashioned against me shall ever prosper. Nothing will hurt or harm me. My faith will not fail. I stand strong through the test; held and helped by the power of the Most High, I am victorious in Him. The elements support my cause; God fights my battles. I am indefatigable, I am strong in the battle, and the angels do my bidding.

The Spirit of the Lord leads and directs me. He leads me from victory to victory. The enemy is defeated and foes are vanquished. I am established triumphantly; my destiny is vindicated. I am a winner. I have divine assistance, because He is my helper, in Jesus name. I believe and I say amen.

Selected Affirmations

I am secure in Jesus, in heaven, far above every power of the enemy. No evil or harm will befall me.

Psalm 91: 10

There shall no evil befall thee, neither shall any plague come nigh thy dwelling.

Isaiah 54: 17

No weapon that is formed against thee shall prosper; and every tongue that shall rise against thee in judgment thou shalt condemn. This is the heritage of the servants of the LORD , and their righteousness is of me, saith the LORD.

Luke 10: 19

Behold, I give unto you power to tread on serpents and scorpions, and over all the power of the enemy: and nothing shall by any means hurt you.

Exodus 14: 13

And Moses said unto the people, Fear ye not, standstill, and see the salvation of the LORD, which he will shew to you today: for the Egyptians whom ye have seen today, ye shall see them again no more forever.

Isaiah 41: 13

For I the LORD thy God will hold thy right hand, saying unto thee, Fear not; I will help thee.

For His Love's Sake

Today I speak over my life and my household that God will show Himself mighty on our behalf. He has overlooked my faults and seen to my need. My desires are granted, and my needs are met; God meets me at every point according to His riches in glory. My life is satisfied with the abundance of His household.

He is my peace. He has broken down every wall of separation, and I have unfettered access to His presence for His loves sake. I am in good health because He has taken away diseases, discomfort, and illnesses. He lives, and I shall live also. My tomorrow is better than my yesterday. The path of the righteous shines brighter and brighter towards the perfect day. I am fulfilled in Him. I increase in greatness; I have comfort on all sides. God is on my side: He has given me grace, I succeed, I am protected, and I increase in the revelation of His power and might. God is my comfort through every trial. I press on like a soldier of the cross. The Word of the Lord is true and real to me. My faith stands strong; I have overcome the world. Good things must happen to me. All things are working together for my good.

God is my life and my salvation; He is the strength of Israel that never lies. He is mighty to save. He leads me on the paths of righteousness for His names sake. I will end my race well. He watches over every step I take. I am not alone. I am surrounded by the host of heaven. I am not forsaken; I am accepted by God for the sake of His Son. I am favoured, I am helped, and I am numbered among the mighty in the land. My life is precious. God is the strength of my life. I am covered by His power. I grow from strength to strength. Nothing holds me down because Gods power has set me free, in Jesus name. I believe and I say amen.

Selected Affirmations

I am in good health because He has taken away diseases, discomfort, and illnesses.

Isaiah 53: 4

Surely he hath borne our griefs, and carried our sorrows: yet we did esteem him stricken, smitten of God, and afflicted.

Romans 8: 28

And we know that all things work together for good to them that love God, to them who are the called according to his purpose.

Proverbs 4: 18

But the path of the just is as the shining light, that shineth more and more unto the perfect day.

Psalm 36: 8

They shall be abundantly satisfied with the fatness of thy house; and thou shalt make them drink of the river of thy pleasures.

Romans 8: 28

And we know that all things work together for good to them that love God, to them who are the called according to his purpose.

His Kingdom and His Will

Today I speak over my life and my household that the kingdom of God is established in our home, and the will of God is in our lives. I have the righteousness, peace, and joy of God. The righteousness of God is established in my life; I have the peace of God like a river; I have joy unspeakable and full of glory.

The will of God is established in my life. I prosper in all I do and in all my ways; my health is restored, and I live in perfect health; my soul prospers in the things of God. He is at work in me, and I will do His good pleasure; my ways are pleasing to Him, and my enemies are at peace with me. Only His will be done in my life; I walk in the power of His presence. Nobody but Jesus has rulership over my life. I receive the influence of the kingdom not made with hands; the power of the eternal kingdom of our God and Christ is at work in my life. The influence of the spirit at work in the sons of disobedience is destroyed in my space and areas of influence. I rise above the works of every other spirit; I establish only the will of God in my life.

Gods Spirit and power have free rein over my life. The flesh and its lusts do not have control over my life. The rule of heaven is established. The influence of hell is destroyed. Wisdom, counsel, might, honour, and power are the pointers of my time. Everything is renewed in my life; nothing stays the same. My change is here. I have a new lease on life. I am established in glory, and I am created for dominion. I have global prominence. This is my season of restoration. All I have lost is given back to me sevenfold. I am a blessed child of God, in Jesus name. I believe and I say amen.

Selected Affirmations

The righteousness of God is established in my life; I have the peace of God like a river; I have joy unspeakable and full of glory.

Isaiah 48: 18

O that thou hadst hearkened to my commandments! then had thy peace been as a river, and thy righteousness as the waves of the sea.

Matthew 6: 10

Thy kingdom come, Thy will be done in earth, as it is in heaven.

Joel 2: 25

And I will restore to you the years that the locust hath eaten, the cankerworm, and the caterpiller, and the palmerworm, my great army which I sent among you.

Proverbs 6: 31

But if he be found, he shall restore sevenfold; he shall give all the substance of his house.

1 Peter 5: 10

But the God of all grace, who hath called us unto his eternal glory by Christ Jesus, after that ye have suffered a while, make you perfect, establish, strengthen, settle you.

Overtaker's Anointing

Today I speak over my life and my household that we have Gods speed in all we do and divine assistance in all our hands find to do.

I am no longer held down; the yoke of delay is destroyed, and every chain of denial is broken. I have divine acceleration, moving swiftly with the overtakers anointing, encountering no roadblocks, no checks. I am jet-propelled into the epicentre of Gods eternal plan for my life. I am aided by the mighty hand of the eternal Creator. My purpose finds fulfilment, and my destiny receives the much-anticipated push in the right direction. I go forward. I march on unhindered. I drop every basket of delay. I cast down every weight that encumbers; I run with ease. I move with angelic assistance and the support of the hosts of heaven. I have the oil of ease. I am helped by many. Nothing is against me. My mark in Christ is sure.

I am strengthened by God; I have grace for the race. I am empowered by the encounter, I will attain, greatness beckons, I am elevated, and God has picked me up. I am numbered with the mighty; my lot with the strong is maintained. The backing of the Lord delivers the unprecedented. I walk in dominion. I am created for good success, and my faith will not fail. I am born again in greatness. I am endued with the seed of greatness. My God is great. Gods goodness gives me the grace that guarantees glorious greatness, in Jesus name. I believe and I say amen.

Selected Affirmations

I cast down every weight that encumbers; I run with ease.

Hebrews 12: 1

Wherefore seeing we also are compassed about with so great a cloud of witnesses, let us lay aside every weight, and the sin which doth so easily beset us, and let us run with patience the race that is set before us.

Deuteronomy 26: 8

And the Lord brought us forth out of Egypt with a mighty hand, and with an outstretched arm, and with great terribleness, and with signs, and with wonders.

1 Kings 18: 46

And the hand of the Lord was on Elijah; and he girded up his loins, and ran before Ahab to the entrance of Jezreel.

Ephesians 3: 16

That he would grant you, according to the riches of his glory, to be strengthened with might by his Spirit in the inner man.

Psalm 16: 5

The Lord is the portion of mine inheritance and of my cup: thou maintainest my lot.

Delivered from Mediocrity

Today I speak over my life and my household that God will nurture us to greatness and that He will perfect everything that concerns me.

I move from where I am to where I ought to be. I engage the positive forces of destiny and enforce every strategy of greatness. I step over every plan to keep me in mediocrity. I run through the troops; I leap over the walls. My fingers are trained for the fight, and my arms are strong enough to bend a bow of steel; my enemies are beaten down, the foes totally discomfited. I rise from the throes of depression and stand on the Rock. I enjoy the full advantage of divine salvation, and I stand on the promises that accompany redemption; I am delivered from smallness, the force of mediocrity is broken, and the chains of limitation and every ceiling of containment are shattered. I outgrow every box of definition and exceed every known expectation. I enforce the power of my destiny: I insist that I will not be limited by the finite walls of the human mind and thought processes. The sky is not my limit; I am seated together with Christ Jesus in heavenly places.

I am free to express purpose to the fullness of Gods infinite power. I operate my life at full capacity. I enforce the blessings of Gods spoken word over my life from creation. I am a fruitful vine; I multiply, I exercise dominion wherever I go, and greatness is guaranteed. I prosper, I have grace, and I walk in the light. I overcome darkness and shine like stars in the night. Nothing can dam the flow of Gods blessing in my life. I live because God is my hope for tomorrow, in Jesus name. I believe and I say amen.

SELECTED AFFIRMATIONS

I am delivered from smallness, the force of mediocrity is broken, and the chains of limitation and every ceiling of containment are shattered. I outgrow every box of definition and exceed every known expectation.

Isaiah 10: 27

And it shall come to pass in that day, that his burden shall be taken away from off thy shoulder, and his yoke from off thy neck, and the yoke shall be destroyed because of the anointing.

Psalm 138: 8

The LORD will perfect that which concerneth me: thy mercy, O LORD, endureth for ever: forsake not the works of thine own hands.

Psalm 18: 29

For by thee I have run through a troop; and by my God have I leaped over a wall.

Ephesians 2: 6

And hath raised us up together, and made us sit together in heavenly places in Christ Jesus.

Genesis 1: 28

And God blessed them, and God said unto them, Be fruitful, and multiply, and replenish the earth, and subdue it: and have dominion over the fish of the sea, and over the fowl of the air, and over every living thing that moveth upon the earth.

Season of Remembrance

Today I speak over my life and my household that God will neither leave nor forsake us. He is my ever-present help in the time of need. His power is available for me at all times; my situation and circumstance change at the mention of His name. I am surrounded by His love. I am shielded by His presence. He is beside me.

My walls are always before Him. I will not fear. Evil will not befall me all the days of my life. God is my sure buckler and my mighty fortress; I will never be shaken. I put my trust in Him; I will never fail. I am led as the sheep of His pasture; I go in and walk out freely, and none shall make me afraid, for I have kept God and His word ever before my eyes. I will not see disgrace. God has honoured me; people will seek my good in the land.

This is my season of remembrance; I flourish like the palm tree. I bring forth fruit in season. I am prepared for greatness; greatness locates me. I have good success. His presence makes the difference. My story has changed, and goodness and mercy chase after me. I see the goodness of the Lord in the land of the living. I stand strong in the Lord and in the power of His might. My faith will not fail; every intimidating entity from hell against my life, career, future, and purpose collapses for His names sake. Darkness has turned to light. I see my way through the light; He is always with me. I am safe, in Jesus name. I believe and I say amen.

SELECTED AFFIRMATIONS

His presence makes the difference. My story has changed, and goodness and mercy chase after me. I see the goodness of the Lord in the land of the living.

Psalm 27: 13

I had fainted, unless I had believed to see the goodness of the LORD in the land of the living.

Psalm 20: 8

They are brought down and fallen: but we are risen, and stand upright.

Psalm 46: 1

God is our refuge and strength, a very present help in trouble.

Isaiah 49: 16

Behold, I have graven thee upon the palms of my hands; thy walls are continually before me.

Psalm 92: 12

The righteous shall flourish like the palm tree: he shall grow like a cedar in Lebanon.

Cross the Mark

Today I speak over my life and my household that the multifaceted blessings of God and His everlasting promises are activated over us. From today, we experience His divine power in every area of our lives.

I cross the mark, and I move into the best season of my life by the prompting of the Holy Spirit. Every grace lined up by God for me is delivered. I encounter the might of God by the freshness of His Word. I am empowered for supernatural breakthroughs. The earth yields her best to me; I achieve the unprecedented and attain unto greatness by the force of the revealed Word of God. Nothing is impossible for me; I have God on my side. I have a living hope, and I have a glorious future; my march towards greatness is sure and consistent. My tomorrow is better than my yesterday, and my path shines brighter to a perfect day. My life is crowned with fatness, my mouth is filled with good things, and God vindicates me.

Life favours me; man honours me. Things work for me. Now I shine forth. My testimony of His goodness is impeccable, and heaven supports my course. The angels hearken to the voice of the Word of God in my mouth. I am established in my place as ordained by God. I am fulfilled in Him. I am strengthened, and success is attracted to me. God is my resource. My faith is strong. I am a blessing to all I encounter. God loves me. I am blessed, in Jesus name. I believe and I say amen.

SELECTED AFFIRMATIONS

I move into the best season of my life by the prompting of the Holy Spirit. Every grace lined up by God for me is delivered. Now I shine forth.

Proverbs 4: 18

But the path of the just is as the shining light, that shineth more and more unto the perfect day.

2 Corinthians 9: 8

And God is able to make all grace abound toward you; that ye, always having all sufficiency in all things, may abound to every good work.

Jeremiah 29: 11

For I know the thoughts that I think toward you, saith the LORD, thoughts of peace, and not of evil, to give you an expected end.

Romans 8: 14

For as many as are led by the Spirit of God, they are the sons of God.

Psalm 126: 2

Then was our mouth filled with laughter, and our tongue with singing: then said they among the heathen, The LORD hath done great things for them.

Reborn into Greatness

Today I speak over my life and my household that God will lift our heads, and He will advance our course in life.

Heaven declares a change in my season and the proclamation of progress has been made. I am jet-propelled into newness of life and unsearchable wisdom from God. My light is come, and time has collided with His chance; I am reborn into greatness as ordained by God. I am a child born in season; things happen for me, and the lines have fallen for me in pleasant places. I leave behind all things pertaining to tears and grief. I have been helped by God and I have the oil of ease. Might and dominion have been granted; I am strong in the Lord and move in His mighty power.

Things have changed for me; nothing is the same. I move up to another level and dimension; I draw water freely from the wells of salvation. I am a star, shining in the midst of darkness. I am a sign, born a wonder to many. Let the earth answer and yield of her increase; let the heaven give of her rains abundantly, let the fountains of the deep be broken up, and let the dry parts of my life be flooded with waters from the river of God. Let wine be given, butter and cheese be released. I work in abundance; I am not limited, in Jesus name. I believe and I say amen.

SELECTED AFFIRMATIONS

Let the earth answer and yield of her increase; let the heaven give of her rains abundantly, let the fountains of the deep be broken up, and let the dry parts of my life be flooded with water from the river of God.

Psalm 67: 6

Then shall the earth yield her increase; and God, even our own God, shall bless us.

Psalm 68: 9

You, O God, did send a plentiful rain, by which you did confirm your inheritance, when it was weary.

Proverbs 3: 20

By his knowledge the depths are broken up, and the clouds drop down the dew.

Psalm 121: 2

My help comes from the LORD, who made heaven and earth.

Psalm 16: 6

The lines are fallen unto me in pleasant places; yea, I have a goodly heritage.

Redeemed by His Blood

Today I speak over my life and my household that Gods abiding presence is with us and makes the difference in our lives. God is with me; I will not fear. His presence is felt around me; I will not be dismayed. My eyes are on Him; I will not see shame.

God is my keeper, God is my shield, God is my strength, and God is my help and helper. My hope is hinged on Him; He will not leave or forsake me. My tomorrow is better than my today. My past is of no negative significance to my destiny. My sins are forgiven, and my transgression is blotted out. The Blood speaks mercy on my behalf. I am established on the path of righteousness. Goodness, mercy, and favour accompany me in my walk. I prosper wherever I turn; I have fullness of joy, I have pleasures in His presence forever, grace delivers the influence of heaven to me, and I am protected and assisted. I am comforted.

I have the oil of ease, and nothing is impossible for me. I hide in the cleft of the rock; no evil eyes shall see me, and no evil hands shall touch me. I am content with the joy of Gods presence. Things can only get better for me. God is for me; nothing is against me. I have life abundant, life eternal. God loves me; He honours me with the joy of His presence, in Jesus name. I believe and I say amen.

Selected Affirmations

My past is of no negative significance to my destiny, my sins are forgiven, and my transgression is blotted out. The Blood speaks mercy on my behalf.

2 Corinthians 5: 17

Therefore if any man be in Christ, he is a new creation: old things are passed away; behold, all things are become new.

1 John 1: 9

If we confess our sins, he is faithful and just to forgive us our sins, and to cleanse us from all unrighteousness.

Isaiah 43: 25

I even I, am he that blots out your transgressions for my own sake, and will not remember your sins.

Hebrews 12: 24

And to Jesus the mediator of the new covenant, and to the blood of sprinkling, that speaketh better things than that of Abel.

Psalm 16: 11

You will show me the path of life: in your presence is fullness of joy; at your right hand there are pleasures forevermore.

Ever-Present Help

Today I speak over my life and my household that God is our shield and ever-present help in the time of need.

The Lord is my defence and my strong tower. He is my light and salvation, The Lord is the strength of my life; I will not fear, nor shall I be afraid. God is faithful to me. He is ever present. He has not left, and He will not leave me; I am inscribed in the palm of His hands. The name of my God is a strong tower; I seek refuge, and I find safety in His name today. His eyes watch over me to keep me from every attack of the enemy. I hide in the fortress of His name and in the shadow of His wings. I invoke the power of His covenant and activate the power of His Blood over every area of my life and my family and insist that my life is secure in Him. I will not be put to shame; I am delivered from disgrace.

I stand complete in Him, and I am forever lifted. My helpers will find me; I have supernatural assistance and angelic support. The hosts of heaven act on my behalf. I have unfettered access to the Throne of Grace; help is not denied in the time of need. I speak peace to every noisy sea and calm to every boisterous storm. I am a survivor! I am in dominion! Created for good success, I am born to win. I exceed every human expectation. God has increased my greatness and comforted me on all sides, in Jesus name. I believe and I say amen.

SELECTED AFFIRMATIONS

The name of my God is a strong tower; I seek refuge, and I find safety in His name today. His eyes watch over me to keep me from every attack of the enemy.

Proverbs 18: 10

The name of the LORD is a strong tower: the righteous runneth into it, and is safe.

Genesis 28: 15

And, behold, I am with thee, and will keep thee in all places whither thou goest, and will bring thee again into this land; for I will not leave thee, until I have done that which I have spoken to thee of.

Psalm 16: 8

I keep my eyes always on the LORD. With him at my right hand, I will not be shaken.

Psalm 103: 20

Bless theLORD , ye his angels, that excel in strength, that do his commandments, hearkening unto the voice of his word.

Hebrews 4: 16

Let us then approach the throne of grace with confidence, so that we may receive mercy and find grace to help us in our time of need (NIV).

Inheritance in Christ

Today I speak over my life and household that Gods ears are open to our cries, and prayers have His attention.

I have not been called to seek Him in vain; my sacrifices are accepted by Him, and my person has not been rejected. God called me and chose me for greatness, I am loved with an everlasting love, and I have been appointed unto amazing things in Him. I have all things that pertain to life and godliness; I am separated unto every good work. God is at work in me both to will and to do of His good pleasure. My eyes behold the brightness of the shining of His word; I do not walk in darkness but have the goodness of the light of His presence. My steps are illuminated and I see my way into greatness. I have the spirit of wisdom and revelation, and I have been blessed with every blessing of God in Christ Jesus. I have received an inheritance in Christ Jesus. I locate the fullness of Gods commanded blessing to me, and I walk therein. The heavens are opened unto me. The keys to the storehouses are in my possession; I increase in the knowledge of His will, I arise in strength, I do exploits, and my generation will hear from me. I walk boldly with power because I have divine access by the power of the Blood of His covenant. I am not condemned; I have been accepted in the beloved, and I have been justified by God through Jesus Christ. I have received mercy through faith in the finished work.

The curse is broken, and the blessing abides eternally. I have abundant life, eternal life, in Christ Jesus. I am seated in heavenly places far above every other power in Christ Jesus. God has restored my original blessings to me. I have dominion; I am created in the image and likeness of God, created unto greatness and good success, in Jesus name. I believe and I say amen.

Selected Affirmations

The curse is broken, and the blessing abides eternally. I have abundant life, eternal life, in Christ Jesus. I walk boldly with power because I have divine access by the power of the Blood of His covenant.

Romans 8: 1

There is therefore now no condemnation to them which are in Christ Jesus, who walk not after the flesh, but after the Spirit.

2 Timothy 1: 7

For God has not given us the spirit of fear; but of power, and of love, and of a sound mind.

Galatians 3: 13

Christ hath redeemed us from the curse of the law, being made a curse for us: for it is written, Cursed *is* every one that hangeth on a tree.

Luke 10: 19

Behold, I give unto you power to tread on serpents and scorpions, and over all the power of the enemy: and nothing shall by any means hurt you.

John 8: 12

Then spake Jesus again unto them, saying, I am the light of the world: he that followeth me shall not walk in darkness, but shall have the light of life.

Seated in Heavenly Places

Today I speak over my life and my household that God will grant us the spirit of wisdom and revelation. I increase in the knowledge of my God and of His will for my life; I walk in light, and my path is flooded with brightness from His presence. I have access to the wealth of wisdom stored up for my emergence as a king-priest. I unlock the doors that lead to the storehouse of the secret riches in the dark places.

I activate His glorious light so I will not grope in darkness. I announce the change; I speak forth that which is written concerning me. I activate angelic support and divine assistance. I take steady steps towards greatness. The eyes of my understanding are enlightened. I see the glory inherent in me. I attain my full potential and fulfil my purpose in Christ Jesus. I am the image and likeness of God, I carry the breath and the Spirit of God, and I am the zenith of His creation. I am on a higher plane; I am seated in heavenly places, and I rise above the contrary powers.

My case is different; I have the life of God, and I have the mind of Christ. As He is, so am I in this world; nothing is impossible for me. I am a believer, and my faith will not fail. My testimony is intact. I cannot be stranded. God is on my side, with no limits, no boundaries. I walk in increase, in Jesus name. I believe and I say amen.

Selected Affirmations

The eyes of my understanding are enlightened. I see the glory inherent in me, and I attain my full potential and fulfil my purpose.

Ephesians 1: 18

The eyes of your understanding being enlightened; that ye may know what is the hope of his calling, and what the riches of the glory of his inheritance in the saints.

Ephesians 1: 21

Far above all principality, and power, and might, and dominion, and every name that is named, not only in this world, but also in that which is to come.

1 Corinthians 2: 16

For who hath known the mind of the Lord, that he may instruct him? but we have the mind of Christ.

Genesis 1: 26

Then God said, Let us make mankind in our image, in our likeness, so that they may rule over the fish in the sea and the birds in the sky, over the livestock and all the wild animals, and over all the creatures that move along the ground.

Job 22: 28

Thou shalt also decree a thing, and it shall be established unto thee: and the light shall shine upon thy ways.

My Confidence and Protection

Today I speak over my life and my household that God will protect us. He will maintain my lot. I will not fall prey to the enemy, and He will not give me over to the will of my enemies; the Lord is my shield, my buckler, and my strong tower. He is my fortress; I will never be shaken. My walls stand strong because He is with me; my foes are defeated round about.

Affliction shall not arise a second time. The battle is the Lords; He fights my battle, and I hold my peace because He is mighty in battle. My enemies fall before the God of the whole earth, and I have the victory. The Lord upholds me by the power of His righteous right hand. I see the Lords goodness in the land of the living. I am made in His image, in the likeness of the great and only God. My life is kept in the safety of His tabernacle. I have the spirit of faith, and fear is defeated.

The Lord is my light and my salvation. He is the strength of my life; whom shall I fear, and of whom shall I be afraid? I denounce the spirit of slavery to fear; I activate the spirit of power, of love, and of a sound mind. I activate the mind of Christ. I have wisdom that is from above. I have the fear of God, in Jesus name. I believe and I say amen.

Selected Affirmations

I denounce the spirit of slavery again to fear; I activate the spirit of power, of love, and of a sound mind. I activate the mind of Christ.

2 Timothy 1: 7

For God has not given us a spirit of fear, but of power and of love and of a sound mind.

Romans 8: 15

For ye have not received the spirit of bondage again to fear; but ye have received the Spirit of adoption, whereby we cry, Abba, Father.

Psalm 18: 2

The LORD is my rock, and my fortress, and my deliverer; my God, my strength, in whom I will trust; my buckler, and the horn of my salvation, and my high tower.

Psalm 27: 1

The LORD is my light and my salvation; whom shall I fear? the LORD is the strength of my life; of whom shall I be afraid?

The Power of His Word

Today I speak over my life and my household that the truth of Gods word will create a buffer for us from the onslaught of the enemy. I dwell in safety because of the power of His word. I have light on my path and a lamp unto my feet. I do not walk in darkness; I will not stray or get off the mark.

I keep the word of God constantly before my eyes; my ways are pleasing unto the Lord. I keep the commandments of the Lord before me, and wisdom is delivered to me. I have length of days and joy unspeakable, full of glory. My paths yield butter and wine. I find fulfilment in all I do. My meat is not denied me, and I find the bone of my own bones. Struggles end and frustrations cease; I enter into the zone of possibilities. I access my area of ease, and this is my season of divine validation.

The command has been given. I activate the voice of the Holy One. These are the days of my appointments. My wait is over, and my change is announced. My season of deliverance is here, and the things that accompany salvation are released to me. I receive the fullness of Gods blessing; I am elevated to the place of greatness and find my place among the princes of the land. I am established with the mighty as it is written of me. Things turn around for my good supernaturally; power and dominion are signs of my days. I prosper. I give succour to many, in Jesus name. I believe and I say amen.

Selected Affirmations

My meat is not denied me, and I find the bone of my own bones.

I activate the voice of the Holy One. These are the days of my appointment. My wait is over, and my change is announced. My season of deliverance is here, and the things that accompany salvation are released to me.

John 8: 32

And you shall know the truth, and the truth shall make you free.

Psalm 119: 105

Your word is a lamp unto my feet, and a light unto my path.

Matthew 2: 6

And you Bethlehem, in the land of Judah, are not the least among the princes of Judah: for out of you shall come a Governor that shall rule my people Israel.

Hebrews 4: 3

Now we who have believed enter that rest, just as God has said, So I declared on oath in my anger, They shall never enter my rest.

Job 14: 14

If a man dies, shall he live again? all the days of my appointed time will I wait, till my change come.

About the Author

Goke Coker is a passionate lover of people and an enthusiastic follower of God. His life is a glowing testimony of Gods unfailing love, amazing grace, and incomparable ability to transform an ordinary boy into an extraordinary significant man.

His early years were marked with tests and temptations that accompany street life in Ojuelegba, a part of Lagos, Nigeria, which was at that time besmirched with a variety of social ills, including gang violence, riotous living, and significant idolatry. The turning point in his life was his encounter with Jesus Christ, which has since blossomed into an affectionate and exemplary relationship. Having been tried in the furnace of diverse challenges, one of which was waiting on God for the fruit of the womb for over a decade and half, his faith in God has been rewarded, as he and his wife have been blessed with a baby girl. He encourages others by sharing proven principles of faith and patience. His life-changing teachings are laced with gripping stories of his personal tests and triumphs.

A licensed minister of the Gospel, Goke serves as a Senior Associate Pastor with the House on the Rock under the leadership of The Reverend Paul Adefarasin, Senior Pastor and Founder of the Ministry.

He lives in Lagos with his family.

Other books:

God 'fessions

Daily Confession of God's Word and Promises over your life.